Our Living Heritage

Michael Joslin

The Overmountain Press
JOHNSON CITY, TENNESSEE

All photographs were taken in
Western North Carolina by
Michael Joslin.

ISBN 1-57072-079-7
Copyright © 1998 by Michael Joslin
All Rights Reserved
Printed in the United States of America

2 3 4 5 6 7 8 9 0

Dedication

*To Cleo Edwards, Howard Burleson, Max Hopson,
Garrett Hopson, Gladys Campbell, Dewey Barnett, and
Garlan Hughes, whose lives were mountains
I have stood upon.*

Table of Contents

Foreword

The title of this new book by Michael Joslin could not be more appropriately named, considering the fact that "heritage" is defined by *Webster's Unabridged* as, "That which is inherited or passed from generation to generation,; hence the lot, condition or status into which one is born; birthright; as liberty of speech is the heritage of freemen." There's a funny thing about a "heritage," though—it doesn't exist until it is recognized and appreciated.

Vulnerable to change, a heritage is easily lost or forgotten and, once dead, is impossible to resurrect. Much depends on memory and a good deal of selective attention, a caring about the past. In this volume of days and ways gone by, as in his previous books and many excellent articles and splendid photographs in the *Johnson City Press*, Michael Joslin shows that our heritage in Southern Appalachia is not so much preserved—a term that reminds me of funeral homes and museums—but one that is alive and well, a "living heritage." In his stories Joslin makes us see, in the words of William Faulkner, that "the past is not even past."

There are several reasons for the vitality of Joslin's reporting. First of all, what he writes about is real, and nothing proves the present so much as reality itself. We know that Joslin has seen the places he describes and has talked to the fascinating people that populate his pieces. His sources are primary. With every article we come away with a sense of lived life in a particular place. In the photographs in his columns we often see the faces of those he interviews, but their words in print are proof enough of authenticity. We hear their voices, as, for example in a piece called "Old Mill," the voice of Warren Campbell who speaks in the presence of his ten-year-old grandson Blake: "My granddaddy, Rev. Dave Campbell, he was a preacher. He died in 1956. He was 102 years old. I'm 75 year old, and the mill was there first time I can remember anything. The waterwheel was made out of wood with cast iron gears. All the pulleys were wood, too." This voice and others recorded herein belong to those who shaped our heritage.

We applaud reporters like Joslin, much in the tradition of Charles Kuralt, for what we call their sense of discovery and exploration in finding items of "human interest" off the so-called beaten track and bringing them to our attention, for making what is old seem almost new. What good writers often do, though, is not so much discover as rediscover or simply remind, to point to what has been before us and around us all along. The obvious we all see eventually, but usually it takes a poet, artist (photographer or painter), or writer to open our eyes to what is worthy of notice around us. They make us see, as Emily Dickinson said, "things overlooked" before.

Certainly Joslin is well aware of the devouring nature of time, and none of his pieces deny that feature of it. Instead of isolating cultural phenomena in an archival fashion, though, he shows the interpenetration of past and present so that what emerges in the pictures he paints of people and places is a realistic sense of change rather than a lament for a romanticized past on the one hand or a deprecation of what we normally call progress on the other. Neither stance will serve us well in the long run, and it is not the function of the reporter to belabor such issues. It may well be, as Henry David Thoreau says, that we have improved our houses but not the people living in them, but such a condition, if it is true, would not seem to be attributable to electricity or indoor plumbing. One's "heritage" probably has less to do with material progress than we normally think. It has a great deal to do with traditional values, independence, self-reliance, love of freedom, neighborliness, and remembering, all amply illustrated in these pages.

If Joslin makes no effort to isolate the past, neither does he attempt to isolate the region. Rather he shows interplay of outside and inside forces constantly at work, the outside elements of change usually appearing victorious over the old ways but ironically highlighting those ways so that their worth in human terms can be better understood and appreciated, the devotion to quality, for example, as seen in several articles dealing with crafting, smithing, milling, or mountain farming, wherever folk took pride in what they did. Also abounding in these pieces is a sense of history, as in the magnificent piece called "Iron Mountain Gap." Near this gap in 1854, according to Frederick Law Olmstead, there was a sign which read: "TOEBIOM, (to Eliza-Bethon 10 miles.)" Not only do Joslin's essays educate us and make us see familiar ground in a new and different way, but they also delight us and entertain us too—a winning combination.

There is a joke in science fiction circles that goes something like this: A captain of a space ship lost in a galaxy goes to his computer and asks: "Where are we?" The computer answers, "In reference to what?" One answer the captain could make to such a question, though it might be difficult for a computer to comprehend, would be, "In reference to our heritage." As we boldly enter into the third millennium, C. E., Michael Joslin is doing what he can to make sure that we not merely remember our heritage, but actually keep it alive.

Robert J. Higgs
Professor Emeritus
East Tennessee State University

Home Comfort cookstove lies abandoned in pasture.

PIECES OF THE PAST

Much of the history of the Southern Appalachians is written on the face of the land. Remnants of those who have lived and died on the mountains clearly tell the story of their lives for those with eyes to see and patience to piece the tale together.

On the steep slopes above Greasy Creek in Mitchell County lie many pages of the history of those who settled there, throve, and perished. Discarded wood cookstoves, neatly stacked piles of rocks, rusting metal drums, collapsed and standing wood structures all speak of the past.

A Home Comfort cookstove overlooks the narrow valley from its place among the rocks and goldenrod stems in a high pasture. Made by the Wrought Iron Range Company of St. Louis, Missouri, the relic speaks of split kindling and crackling fires to cook an old-time dinner of soup beans, corn bread, and maybe a fat pullet from the farm flock.

In the winter it provided a welcome addition to the heat from a fireplace or heating stove. In the summer sweat popped on the brow of the farm wife while she cooked roasting ears and trout fresh from the creek. It won't say clearly why or how it got way up in the pasture when it was retired, replaced by a newfangled electric or gas stove. It might be there to slow the rush of spring floods running down the creek, a job many rock piles performed.

Neatly constructed piles of rock can be found throughout the mountains. On Greasy Creek they fill depressions in pastures and stretch across gulleys deep in the woods, pieces of forest that once were pastures or cornfields.

Early mountain farmers found fertile ground, but that soil was thickly strewn with rocks ranging from pebbles to good-sized boulders. Each plowing season the rocks were gathered as they obstructed the plow point, and were moved to places where the freshets of spring threatened to wash away the fields. The rock ricks became permanent fixtures as the soil piled against their backs and gravity anchored them in place.

Harnessing and controlling the water required mountain ingenuity. Getting water from the spring at first required buckets and manpower, but as folks settled in, gravity was used to bring the water closer to the house, or even into it.

Near the old stove on Greasy Creek is a rusting 55-gallon drum. About twenty feet above it is a carefully constructed spring box with a pipe running out of it to the drum. Another pipe leaves the bottom of the drum and disappears beneath the soil.

In times past, that old drum was the water reservoir for a household. The lower pipe carried the sweet spring water either into the house or into a springhouse where it was used to cool milk and butter as well as for drinking water, saving a hike up the hill.

Near the head of Greasy Creek, a small farmstead lies above the dirt road on a narrow shelf of land under a steeply

Buildings of old Murphy homestead stand.

climbing ridge. A stout barn, several outbuildings, spring-house, and the main house itself still stand in good condition, the chestnut boards weathering time well.

The wooden barn with its hayloft, stalls, and mangers speaks of the livestock that served the mountain folks for food, transportation, and labor. The barn stands beside the narrow driveway that climbs to it from the main road, itself narrow and rutted.

Next to the barn is another wooden building that served to store food for both man and beast. A large corncrib forms one side, the laths and open spaces making tiger stripes as the setting sun shines through them.

Only the hinges remain of most of the various doors and hatches on the outside of this tin-roofed structure. One door with a ladder nailed to its front stands whole, except for a missing board. Inside, a clutter of canning jars—some empty, some with lids and contents intact—lies on the floor with the broken shelving that once supported them. Torn pieces of corrugated cardboard hang in places on the walls, remnants of the home-style insulation that protected the canned goods from the cold.

Beside this storage building a small stream flows. Twenty feet or so above are the collapsed remains of what was probably the outhouse, built over the water so the wastes would be carried away to the main creek. This practice contributed to the health problems of many twentieth century mountain folks as the quality of the water deteriorated.

A bit farther upstream is the old springhouse, built right by the spring box formed from rock and mortar. Concrete troughs inside held the clean cold water before it overflowed to run downhill and flush the outhouse.

Right beside the springhouse is the main dwelling place. The kitchen door once opened to the building that served as refrigerator and water source. The porch has fallen in places and is rotting in others. A thriving ash tree has pushed its way through the boards to seek the light above, curving gracefully under the roof.

Supported by locust posts and rock piers, the house itself stands as solid as the day its sills were laid. The rocks piled

Old jars clutter floor of storage building.

to form the piers do not appear to form a secure base, but their longevity tells of mountain ingenuity and precision and the ability to make do with materials at hand.

Just inside the kitchen door two round holes show where the cookstove pipe ran though the wall to the brick chimney which lies collapsed outside. Through the empty window frames can be seen the rich green-gold moss covering the red bricks that still form sections of the fallen chimney.

No pane remains intact. Shattered glass lies inside and out, telling of hunters and rock-throwing boys who couldn't resist the glitter of windows on the abandoned house.

The chestnut boards are sound throughout the house. Layers of cardboard show the attempt to shut out the cold winter winds, and tattered strips of wallpaper—faded roses on faded trellises—tell of a love for beauty.

The bedrooms are small, eight feet square, and the living room not much larger. A central chimney with a flue opening reveals that a heating stove provided winter comfort. The broad porch that wraps around the front and the kitchen side of the house speaks of cool summer evenings after days of hot work.

A woman's dress shoe and a heelless brogan remain to hint at the genders and sizes of the folks who once dwelt here at the head of Greasy Creek. But some pages of this book are blank, needing to be filled in by the memories of those who remain.

Greasy creek: homestead - pretty
& Chimney
& porch
outhouse - leads to
& main crea
barn - hay loft,
stalls
= food,
transportation
labor

The community of Buladean lies ringed by mountains.

WILDER MINE

At the top of a steep ridge running from Iron Mountain, a large scooped hole overlooks the headwaters of Greasy Creek. Saplings stretch skyward from the leaf-filled bottom of the cup-shaped depression, and a large oak with a shattered crown anchors the top right side.

Today it is a quiet, lonely spot visited rarely by hunters and their game. The only sounds are the wind whistling through the trees and rustling the leaves or the high-pitched scream of a red tailed hawk.

A hundred years ago it was the noisy scene of daily activity, as work-hardened mountain men using hand tools gouged magnetic iron ore from its hiding place on the ridge. The small opening belies the great importance that the mine had for the community that lay at the mouth of Greasy Creek.

In many ways, the history of the mine is the history of Buladean, a rural community tucked between Roan Mountain and Iron Mountain.

In the first place, the name "Buladean" has not always identified the community. At least two names have preceded this one. The first was "Wilder." The community was known by the name of the famous Union General who became a developer in the region that his troops had traversed during the Civil War.

General John T. Wilder is best known in this area as the owner of the Cloudland Hotel and the Roan on which it perched. Less known is the fact that at one time or another in the latter part of the nineteenth century he owned much of the land that the Roan overlooks.

Wilder invested much time and effort in developing mining and railroading enterprises in the East Tennessee and Western North Carolina area. In Johnson City he built a large blast furnace to process the output from his various mines.

In what is now Buladean, he established a forge—known as Wilder's Forge—which gave the community its name for

Paul Garland holds old documents.

several years. The name "Wilder" is kept alive in a few memories even today.

"General Wilder owned all the mountain. This little valley was named for him," says Paul Garland, former principal of Buladean Elementary School and a lifelong resident of the area.

Garland is uncertain of dates, but he is sure of the name, because his father was the postmaster for many years as well as the general storekeeper. As such he was the repository of valley lore.

"My father was so good; he knew all the stuff about the history and land around here. He told me a lot, but I should have found out more before he died," says Garland as he leafs through old documents he has collected during his eight decades as a resident under the Roan.

Sometime late in the 1800s, the name changed from "Wilder" to Magnetic City as the valley took its name from the mineral resource that flowed from the veins on the mountain.

"I don't know when, but I do know it was known as Wilder, then it was named Magnetic City. When they changed the name, they moved the Post Office up to Rock Creek, above where Odom's Chapel Road now stands," says Garland, pointing up towards Hughes Gap.

A bulletin published by the State of Tennessee in 1923, *The Magnetic Iron Ores of East Tennessee and Western North Carolina* by W.S Bayley, describes the mines open above Greasy Creek in a section on "Magnetic City Prospects." Bayley also gives an analysis of the ore.

According to the late Howard Burleson, who lived most of his life on Greasy Creek, mining ceased at the head of the creek when the mine shaft caved in one night. The workers habitually stored all their tools in the shaft when they quit work each night, so the mine was effectively closed by the roof fall.

It was never reopened. Buried beneath tons of rock and earth and decades of leafmold lie the well-worn tools wielded by the miners of Magnetic City.

Children explore depression where old mine stood.

When the mining ceased and the forge went cold, residents clamored to have the post office moved once more to the valley floor in the center of the community.

"When they decided it was wrong and they moved the post office back here, they asked for names to give it. We had a teacher at the Presbyterian Church School who liked the song 'Beulah Land.' She wanted to call it that.

"But a man from Tennessee came over and told us they had a town named 'Buladean' there. It's a Scotch-Irish name. 'Bula' means 'beautiful, lovely,' and 'dean' means 'hills.' So that was the name they chose—'Buladean,'" says Paul Garland.

Garland remembers playing as a boy among the debris left by the forge. Large wheels and rocks lay by the creek. When he grew up and became a teacher, he took his students up to the old mine.

"I took my class up and we checked pieces of ore with a magnet. We brought some big pieces back to the classroom, but over the years they disappeared," says Garland, remembering the steep climb and the eager children recovering pieces of their heritage under his tutelage.

Researching his community's past has been a lifelong quest for Paul Garland.

He has an old postcard with a picture of the church and the name "Magnetic City, N.C." printed across it. He has old letters and other yellowing documents. He can see old wooden homes from a prosperous past crumbling to ruin. He has his memories, many of which are secondhand from the generations before his.

The valley has undergone surface changes, just as its name has changed from Wilder to Magnetic City to Buladean. No longer does mining pay the bills. Farming continues, but it is usually supplemented by outside jobs.

Yet the Roan towers above, and the rocks stand firm below as they have from time immemorial. The lone depression above Greasy Creek remains mute testimony of Magnetic City days.

named first wilder bc general wilder owned all the land. then magnetic City because it was a big mining city. The mine collapsed and never reopened. Buladean became its new name bc it means beautiful hills. The community is supported by farming and outside jobs

Large rock wall snakes through bottomland off Odom's Chapel Road.

WALLS

And some are loaves and some so nearly balls
We have to use a spell to make them balance:
"Stay where you are until our backs our turned!"
We wear our hands rough with handling them.
                    "Mending Wall" by Robert Frost

Throughout Southern Appalachia you can find them—prodigious piles of rock wedded to form walls.

Some of the walls are short, some long. Some are knee-high, some tower overhead. Many seem to be the work of a vanished race, for they stand without apparent purpose in the midst of the forest.

Yet all have been made by men and women. Hardworking farmers and their families moved mountains of rock to clear fields, to stop erosion, or to stem floods. The impressive piles endure as monuments to their labor and their love of the land.

Up Odom's Chapel Road a long dark wall snakes across a rich bottomland, one of the largest flat fields in the Buladean community. It curves in places and cuts across at a right angle on one end, but it doesn't appear to wall anything in or out.

The wall is decorative in its rugged mass, yet only the most dedicated artist would have spent the amount of time and energy such a structure would demand for completion. And it is set in an isolated cove that few people ever visit.

Who built it and why?

"If I understand it right, old man Anderson Hughes built that rock wall, started on it. Later on after he died, his boy

Mitchell Joslin stands at base of large rock wall that forms a terrace high in the woods above Creasy Creek. Warren Campbell mowed hay here as a boy.

Rob continued building the rock wall. It was to get the rocks out of the field.

"Rob had a peg leg—a wooden leg—and he had a blind horse. He'd load those rock on an old sled, and the horse would drag them to the wall," says Warren Campbell, whose father purchased the field after the wall was built.

Campbell sits in his harness shop on Blevins Branch Road talking with an old friend, Junior Street. Horse talk has turned to talk of rock walls, as they discuss how the "untelling" number of rocks in the fields had to be gathered into piles to clear the way for cultivation. Specific memories arise.

"I remember I got scared to death once along that rock fence. I'd never been out there before, and I walked a girl out there one night," says Street, ducking his head, which wears a hint of a blush.

"There was a big old white horse came up just a-snorting. I didn't know they even had a horse. I never wanted to go back in there again," he says, as a grin splits his friend's face.

Besides serving as depositories for troublesome rocks or convenient shelters for courting, the rock walls stopped erosion in the steep fields. At the top of Blevins Branch Road, one pasture wears a series of walls from top to bottom.

The walls look like military redoubts, but instead of protecting soldiers from losing their lives from gunfire, they protected the field from losing its rich soil to rain.

"They placed them walls where they had swags in the holler. That kept them from washing and got rid of the runoff," says Campbell, demonstrating with his hands how the walls would interrupt the flow of soil-laden water.

In exceptionally steep coves the rock walls trapped so much runoff that terraces built from the loose soil. On Greasy Creek, where Campbell grew up many years ago, there is one cove with a series of walls that have grown into giant steps.

Some are up to twelve feet tall and stretch sixty feet or more across the cove. Their purpose has been lost in the shadows of tall trees. The stacked rocks wear coats of moss

A series of walls prevents erosion in pasture at top of Blevins Branch Road.

and ferns and appear as relics of a lost civilization under the thick forest that has grown on and around them.

"The water would come down that field and build up the soil behind. I mowed all in there. I've been married this fifty-four years past, and I mowed in there before I was married. It's been that long ago," says Campbell, as he rises from his stool and walks to the open door.

He points across the tobacco fields to a steep wooded ridge that rises in the distance.

"Right up there, see through that tree where the ridge runs down? That's where that cove is. It was all cleared when I was a boy," he says, measuring his life by the size of the trees that have sprouted, grown to saplings, and matured along with him.

The origin of some walls needs to be traced back through the generations. They form permanent memorials to the past.

Mike Honeycutt of Johnson City appreciates the beauty of the old rock walls along the creek on his Buladean property that once belonged to his grandfather. One wall curves along the inside of the creek, forming a protective barrier between the water and the barns and other buildings of his homeplace.

"I think it was just a place to put rocks, just picking up rocks from the field. I don't think that flooding was a big deal. My grandfather Garrett Honeycutt built it," says Honeycutt, as he shows his fiancee, Patty, the structures of his heritage.

"My grandfather graduated from Milligan in 1890, and he taught school on Greasy Creek and Beans Creek, in the old one-room schoolhouses. He worked on the walls to clear the fields in the summer.

"They sure are pretty," says Honeycutt, admiring both the industry and the rugged beauty of his ancestor's work.

Like many aspects of the Appalachian past, building rock walls is largely a bygone art. An occasional immigrant will have the money to pay for the time and effort such a structure demands, but most mountain folks have neither the time nor need to clear large pieces of land.

The walls remain to tell of a time when the size of the effort was not measured in dollars, but in the resulting benefit to the land and its people.

Walls benefited land & people by clearing fields, stopping erosion, or to stopp flooding. There is no need for them now so they are nice art.

This old photograph adorns the tomb of Rev. Dave Campbell and his wife. He established the mill in the 1800s.

OLD MILL

The older generation of mountain folks have seen remarkable changes in their homeland over the course of their lives. One way of life has largely passed, giving way to a modern lifestyle that differs little from that of their peers across the country.

Their memories hold the clearest records of those bygone days when independence and self-reliance meant more than an attitude; they were literal reality. Each community was self-sustaining.

An important part of the isolated coves was the mill that ground the corn, wheat, buckwheat, and rye into meal or flour, the basic stuff of the staff of life. For generations, mountain families routinely carried their pokes of grain to the neighborhood mill, leaving a toll in kind and departing with sacks smoking with meal dust.

On Greasy Creek in Mitchell County, the Campbell family operated a water-powered mill from sometime in the second half of the 1800s until the mid-twentieth century. The older Campbells remember those days well.

"From the time I was big enough to do anything at all, I'd help them grind, from the time I was as big as that boy until they quit grinding," says Warren Campbell, pointing to his ten-year-old grandson Blake, who sits watching *The Mask* cartoon this Saturday morning.

The Campbells' mill was set up to run on the water power of Greasy Creek. A dam held the water back until it rose to the height of the flume, or millrace, a wooden trough which ran down to the waterwheel that powered the mill, located beside the creek above the Campbell homeplace.

"My granddaddy, Rev. Dave Campbell, he was a preacher. He died in 1956. He was 102 years old. He bought the mill to start with back in the 1800s, then he give it to my daddy when he got married.

"I'm seventy-five year old, and the mill was there first time I can remember anything. The waterwheel was made out of wood with cast iron gears. All the pulleys were wood, too," says Warren, a millwright for many years who has always maintained his home in Buladean.

The old mill ground mountain grains, but mostly corn. People arrived at all times of the day, so each of the Campbells from the grandmother to the young boys was skilled in the operation of the mill.

"They'd come from miles with a sack of corn across a mule or a horse. We'd take a toll out, take a half gallon of corn out of a bushel. Daddy had a box; he take it out before it was ground. He wouldn't heap it up; he'd take his hand and rake over it," says Warren, demonstrating with his hand how they would take only their fair share.

The operation of the mill still remains clear in his mind from the many times he either watched or ground by himself.

"There was an adjustment where you adjust it fine or coarse. It had a little lever. Pull the lever up—set to coarse or fine—then lock the lever back.

"You put the corn in the hopper. When the mill run, it shook the corn down into the rocks (the millstones). The shelled corn would run down in a steady stream," says Warren, showing how the hopper shook back and forth to funnel down the grain.

The power came from the creek water running through the flume to the wheel. The time needed to grind a bushel of corn varied.

"That there depends on how much water there was running in the creek. In the summertime when the water was low, it'd take about an hour.

"You had a water gate. If you could run four inches through that flume, you could grind in about twenty to thirty minutes. My grandmaw, she'd go up there and set. She'd set that mill up and go to sleep while it was grinding," says Warren. "It ground slow, that waterwheel did."

Warren's sister Bertie Ledford remembers the mill, too. She still lives in sight of the creek and can take you to the sites of the dam and the mill.

"I was three years younger than Warren, but I remember it

Greasy Creek foams down a small waterfall at the former site of the old dam.

just as good as if it was yesterday," she says as she leads the way down a narrow, snow-covered trail dotted with dog paw prints. Above the creek she points to a small waterfall beside a large rock outcrop.

"That's where the dam was," she says, describing how it held back the water to fill the flume.

A couple of hundred yards down the creek she stops at the site where the mill formerly stood. A flat place by the creek and a few stacked rocks are all that remain.

"I know it was here because I'd walk up that path from the house," Bertie says, pointing to the old homeplace down the creek.

"I would come down with Granny and she'd pour the corn in. Then she'd turn the water on the wheel. After she'd get done she'd always cover up the hopper," she says, her eyes sparkling behind her glasses.

The mill served the community for many years. Warren's son Bobby Campbell remembers it from his childhood.

"I was just a little feller when they pulled it out in '49 or '50. I was six or seven years old. I remember the building and the dust—flour and meal dust everywhere," says Bobby, one of the last generation to experience that essential part of the Appalachian heritage.

Warren Campbell knows the role of the mill during its heyday, for he lived it.

"That mill was good for the community. I've seen that mill run all day, from early in the morning to late in the evening, with everything from a peck to a meal sack full. Old people, they'd come bring a turn of corn, then stay and eat dinner," says Warren.

"Sometime I wish times was back then," says his wife, Gladys, remembering the way life was before they were caught up in the hurly-burly of modern life.

As time passed, flour and meal could be cheaply purchased at the general stores in the Buladean community. The mill became less and less necessary and began to deteriorate.

First the mill wheel rotted, to be replaced by an old Chevrolet engine, then Warren's daddy moved up to Rock

Creek, taking the mill with him.

"The last it was run was somewhere along in the '60s. He had a gasoline motor then," says Warren.

"A Jeep motor," says Bobby, remembering time spent with his grandfather. "He used it to crush corn for chicken feed for a long time."

"Then the motor locked up on my daddy," says Warren. "The mill hasn't been used since."

The flume rotted down; then the old mill building. Now only rocks remain to tell the tale of the community mill— rocks, and the Campbells who were there.

L-R: Bobby Campbell, Warren Campbell, and Gladys Campbell remember the old mill.

rev dave campbell built the mill that ran on creek water w/ a dam to run. they did flour, corn (meal). It helped the community but died when you could buy more products in a general store.

Frank Whitson leans on his pitchfork while feeding an Angus-Hereford cow by his old homeplace.

WHITSON'S HOMEPLACE

"It was about the prize place there was around," says Frank Whitson, looking up at the faded white paint on his old homeplace on Beans Creek in the Buladean community of Mitchell County.

He has seen many changes in this mountain community since his birth in 1909. A way of life that revolved around family and farm has given way to one that involves work and cash money. Yet Whitson holds on to many of the traditions he grew up with.

He continues to farm, raising cattle and tobacco and putting up large quantities of hay each year. He owns more land in his native Mitchell County than any other man and finds comfort in that.

It's something he learned from his father, Sam Whitson.

"My daddy owned more tracts of land than anyone in the county. All my people was land thirsty. I'd rather invest in land than anything else in the world," he says, looking around the narrow valley where his view is bounded on all sides by land he owns, land that at one time was his father's.

His eyes rest on a broad piece of bottom-land across the creek from the aging house. He sweeps his hand toward it.

Whitson looks over the interior of his old home.

"That's about the largest piece of creek bottomland in Mitchell County. Mallory Griffith—used to work for the agriculture people—measured it and told me," says Whitson as he replaces his hand on the pitchfork he has been using to throw hay to his Angus-Hereford cattle.

He leans forward, supporting himself on the pitchfork, letting his memories return to the early decades of the century. He remembers his father and the large family that lived in the "prize house" of Buladean.

"My daddy bought this house and barn on January 17, 1907. He paid $2,500; I got the deed. That date turned out to be my birthday two years later," says Whitson. leading the way into the back wing of the large house.

Rocks hold the tin roof down in places, and a column or two are askew. The porch sags here and there. But the door opens easily enough into a large room.

"I was the youngest boy of his first wife. There were four-teen of us. He married another woman and had ten more. I used to sleep right there on what they called a lounge," says Whitson, pointing to a place near the wall.

"I'd build fires in the winter early in the morning. Used to, the chickens was the clock. The rooster'd crow, and you got up.

"One morning I heard a rooster and got up and built a fire. It was just a-roaring, but it was only midnight. I tried to tell my daddy that I'd heard the rooster, but he didn't believe me," says Whitson, as he turns to walk to the front of the house.

His mother died when he was four-and-a-half years old. His father remarried "on my birthday again, January 17, 1915." Life continued for the large family.

Upstairs on the bedroom walls there is mute evidence of the children's activities. Schoolwork and names are scrawled

Frank Whitson picks up a grain cradle to give it a swing.

in chalk on the dark boards. The names of two sisters, Ethel and Polly, stand out clearly, along with spelling lessons and math.

Raising enough to feed the large family took an effort from all, but they were always successful. Their life was hard, but the food was bountiful.

"We always had plenty of everything you could grow on a farm. We'd take cabbage and make a keg of kraut. We got bushels upon bushels upon bushels of beans. My daddy used to grow more corn than any man in this county," he says. He points out the window to a large wooden building with a loft and corncribs.

"Those cribs hold 500 bushels of corn apiece. Daddy'd hire help and pay them in corn and pork. I've known him to kill as many as eleven fat hogs in one season. They wanted that bacon—sow bosom I call it—and corn. They wanted something to eat.

"You know, they say that pork is bad for you, and I agree and tell them that pork killed my daddy. He eat it every day of his life. It finally got him, though, at last. He was ninety-five year and nine month old. Why, he would have made it to a hundred if he'd never eat pork," says Whitson. He starts to smile.

"I just can't work, can't do nothing without meat. These here vegetarians, all they do is talk. I like that streaked meat—sow bosom I call it. This morning I had me some with a couple of eggs," he says, his light eyes sparkling behind his glasses.

Work has dominated Whitson's life from the beginning—another tradition inherited from his father.

"I'd say he was the hardest working man that ever was in this area. He bore that name. He was a strong man," he says.

"He never owned a tractor in his life. He raised mules; they went to cotton land in South Carolina. He'd break 'em to work, and I'd break 'em to ride. I been almost killed several times," says Whitson, heading out the door to walk down to an old building standing by the side of the road.

"He made muleshoes and horseshoes out of old wagon

tires. My daddy was the best blacksmith. I would blow for him. I had to stand on a block of wood to pull the balluses, what you call bellows now," says Whitson, pulling off the lock to open the dusty blacksmith shop.

He has already removed the anvil, but the large bellows rests under the board he used to raise up and down to fan the smithy's fires. The fire pit is still clearly defined by rocks, and old wagon tires rust in the back.

Whitson picks up a grain cradle and gives it a tentative swing. His family raised their own wheat on a nearby mountain field, the only one in the area where the crop would thrive.

By the age of ten Whitson was working a team of horses to log the adjacent ridge top.

"Well, I drove a team from the time I was big enough to hold the lines. I drove a snatch team to log that hill over there. It was a big pair of western horses. They'd stomp you, kick you. You had to watch out," he says, pointing across the bottom to a steep ridge.

By fourteen he was hauling timber and telephone poles from Buladean to Toecane, about a twenty-mile round trip that took all day. That's how he earned his first cash.

Whitson left home at fifteen. He worked with wood one way or another. Starting in Erwin, Tennessee, in a lumber and planing mill run by A. R. Brown, by thirty-five he had his own timber company that worked throughout the region. He would set up camp with his workers and stay all week.

"I always built a shack right close to my mills. I'd come home every Friday night. I would feed sixteen men at the table. Keep nine beds. About every way you looked on a moonlight night you could see light. I had a telephone and a Home Comfort cookstove," he says, remembering the many years of hard work that financed his land purchases.

Whitson retired from the timber industry about twenty years ago, but he continues to farm and invest in land. He lives in Buladean and plans to restore his old homeplace.

"Yeah, this is my old home," he says, raking rocks with his pitchfork to keep the water flowing directly down the branch bed.

frank whitson

From the back of the cove stand the Greene log cabin and the Joe Greene house. Farther down is the Barnett house.

STANLEY COVE

Patterns of movement into the Southern Appalachians have been studied for decades, tracing migrations from Pennsylvania, Virginia, North Carolina, and elsewhere. Equally interesting are the patterns of movement of individual families, as they spread from a homeplace into neighboring coves to flourish or fail.

One example of such family growth and decline lies spread along the bottom of a fertile cove that climbs away from the intersection of Big Rock Creek and Little Rock Creek in Mitchell County. Four houses sitting beside a winding branch and a small cemetery resting atop the northern ridge tell the tale of the Stanley family.

The original homeplace has long since crumbled to the ground, the logs returning to the earth from which they sprang. Rickus Stanley built along the banks of Rock Creek and raised his family in the rich bottomland that spreads there.

"Rickus built down over the cliff above the creek. They called it the Rickus Cliff. I remember seeing the house well, but it's been rotted down now at least fifty year," says Frank Whitson, who has lived on parts of the Stanley property for many of his eighty-seven years.

In the cemetery, two large fieldstones mutely honor the family patriarch and his wife. Saplings push from the soil, but vegetation has not yet covered the memorials.

Beside these bare fieldstones stand two monuments with chiseled inscriptions: "Joseph Stanley Born July 20, 1824 Died Feb 2, 1913," reads one, and "Malinda Wife of Joseph Stanley Born Dec 22, 1825 Died May 28, 1906," says the other.

Behind the mouth of the cove below stands a large log house with two rooms attached. This was Joseph's house, built for him by his father. It is a substantial structure, with hewn poplar logs over eighteen inches wide, carefully jointed at dovetailed corners. Two board-and-batten rooms, a kitchen, and a bedroom are attached, one to the back and one to the side.

A large fieldstone chimney and hearth heated the dwelling. A stout ladder-stairs led to the loft, supported on solid beams, where most of the family slept. Layers of paper peel from the walls—feed bags overlain by decorative wallpaper, the only insulation other than the thick logs.

Nearby stands a large barn, shelter for the stock and the feed raised for the animals. Logs form the lower story and the framework for the loft, now covered by warped boards.

About a quarter mile away in the back of the cove, another large log cabin stands. It was the home of one of Joseph Stanley's daughters, Cissy.

"I have a transfer from Joseph Stanley to Cissy Greene. It's no telling how old the house is. Joseph Stanley built it for her when she married a Greene," says Frank Whitson, standing beside the solid structure.

Squared off oak logs form the main room of the house. From the front, the beams of the loft show clearly where their ends protrude through notches in the log that crowns the lower story. This one log is poplar, perhaps used because it was easier to notch for the loft beams.

"They chinked it with mud, clay mud. Daubing they called it," says Whitson, running his hand along the orange-colored chinking.

Whitson believes the logs were hewed with a broadax and a poleax. Scoring marks still show clearly on many of the logs where the builders chopped perpendicularly into the log before slicing along the grain to square the sides.

"I'd say it was just a family affair. They may have been someone in the community to help, to swap off labor. But

Frank Whitson examines the Greene cabin.

they probably just worked on it during rainy days or in the wintertime. It was probably built somewhere in the later half of the 1800s," says Whitson, as he examines the square structure.

Noticing a series of holes bored into the oak logs, he says, "They bored those holes for pegs to hang equipment on."

Between the two log houses are two wood-frame houses. One stands less than fifty yards from the Cissy Greene house, between two large willow trees growing from the banks of the narrow creek. A long porch faces the creek.

"Joe Greene, Cissy's son, built that house. It has sheetrock and hardwood floors. When he built it, he moved out of the old log house into it. When he moved to the mouth of Bad Creek, he sold out to me," says Whitson, looking up at the still-sturdy house, sided with rolled tar paper.

Between this frame house and the first cabin at the mouth of the cove stands another frame house, covered in identical material. Joe Greene's daughter married Henry Barnett, and they built this house about a hundred yards down the cove.

The Barnett house has ceiling tile and wood panelling on the walls. The kitchen floor wears a linoleum cover. A cracked wall mirror reflects the emptiness of the rooms. The porch is concrete. A hand pump sits atop the well box beside the house.

The Barnetts moved out in the 1950s. They were the last of the Stanley family to reside in the cove.

"I wouldn't buy Henry out because I didn't want him to leave. But he sold out to someone else, then I bought it," says Whitson, who now owns the cove from the mouth, where he has built a large rock house, to the back, where the long pasture runs up to the ridge.

The four houses stand empty today, but they speak of times past and the love that bound a family together. Some of the Stanleys still cluster on the ridge top, where the winds of change stir the leaves that blanket the graves.

Stanleys

Many extraordinary views lie along the Bald Road.

OLD BALD (BALL) ROAD

Today, even its name is lost in the obscurity of the past. Some folks call it the Bald Road, others the Ball Road. But whatever its name, this dirt path that rises from the valley floor in Buladean to climb steadily to the crest of Roan Mountain is intertwined with the history of the community and the mountain that rises above it.

The confusion over the name comes from the fact that Bald Road makes perfect sense, while Ball Road is just a name accepted for decades. The Hopson family lived on the road they called "Ball" for several years, and octogenarian Garrett Hopson has lived in and around Buladean most of his life.

"B-A-double-L," said Garrett Hopson emphatically. Then he paused.

"Well, B-A-L-D just might be right. See, on top of the Roan it's naked, except where you get into the timber. It'd be B-A-L-D, Bald for the balds," he said, the light twinkling from his glasses as he nodded his head in acceptance of his own logic.

Since the old road leads to the grass and heath balds of the Roan, the name "Bald" should be correct.

Paul Garland sticks with B-A-L-L as the name of the road.

"B-A-L-L," said Paul Garland, who is a few years older than Garrett and has hiked the Ball Road many times. But he doesn't know how it got that name.

"Well, I don't know. I have no idea," he said when asked why it was named "Ball."

"Why would it be called after a rolling ball when it's named after the bald?" said Warren Campbell, a lifelong Buladean resident who lives near the road. "It wouldn't, would it? I wouldn't think so."

Whatever the correct name, the road links the present to the past, just as it links the valley with the Roan that towers above. Its origin is lost in the mists of time, but its various uses have been preserved.

When the Cloudland Hotel stood on the top of the Roan, the Bald Road provided access for both visitors and those local farmers who supplied the hotel with produce.

"An old black man drove a hack from Johnson City up past my house up to the Garlan Hughes house then up the Ball Road. Mack James was his name, and he would drive all the way up to the Cloudland Hotel," said Paul Garland, drawing on the tales told by his parents and grandparents.

Nearly every native of Buladean has heard tales of the trips their ancestors made carrying goods up to the hotel on the Roan. For many years this was the closest and surest market for just about everything raised on mountain farms or hunted in the woods.

"My grandmother and grandfather used to carry things up to sell. They used to pick blackberries up at home on Greasy Creek and sell them for ten cents a gallon," said Warren Campbell, looking up from a piece of harness he was working.

"People sold vegetables of all kinds, and some would carry chickens up there alive and dressed pigs. Just anything they had to sell they'd take up there," said Vergie Hughes, who has spent her life in Buladean in the shadow of the Roan.

While some farmers might have taken their horses or mules, most made the trip on foot. What seems a mighty trek today was simply a necessary circuit a hundred years ago.

"My mother, when she was just a girl, her mother and daddy would take loads and loads up there just about every day," said Garrett Hopson.

Tales of some legendary feats of hauling have been passed down. There were some mighty stout mountain folks hiking the road in the past.

"Old man Sul Garland. They say he sold somebody a stove and carried it from his house to the top of the Roan on his back," said Warren Campbell.

When the Cloudland Hotel fell into ruin, the Bald Road remained important to the mountain folks who had settled along it on the steep shoulders leading from the Roan.

"When I was a boy they farmed the awfullest sight up in there. Corn, wheat, beans—you'd see no bugs on them. Finest land you've ever seen. Some was steep, some laid very well," said Garrett Hopson, remembering the 1920s.

Starting in the mid-1930s he raised a family along the Bald Road, farming twenty acres of land. He recalls the others who shared the road and a way of life that has disappeared from the higher reaches of the road.

"They was five or six families lived above Junior Ingram's place. The upper house was an old man's, my first wife's granddaddy, Sul Garland," said Hopson, as he ran down the list of names: the Mosleys, Ben and his family; Bill Honeycutt and his sons and daughters; Washington and Maggie Bowman, known as Wash and Mag; and others.

Today, the crumbling ruins of log cabins with the fallen piles of chimney rocks stand as a memorial to these farm families that found a good, full life along the Bald Road. The echoes of creaking wagons and shouting teamsters, the laughter of little children, and the quiet murmur of conversation among travelers on the road have died.

Yet, there is still life along the Bald Road. Hunters, hikers, and horsemen continue to travel the deeply worn roadbed up into the mountains. The opening to the road is off Blevins Branch Road in Buladean. It is wide enough for four-wheel drive trucks there, and the deep ruts testify to its use. The road narrows as it climbs, until high on the shoulders of the ridges, it is a narrow trail winding among large hardwood trees.

Bald Road has sunk over the years.

The change in altitude is often revealed by the change in weather as the road winds its way along the high ridges. While the opening of the road may be warm and clear, the higher reaches can be covered with an inch or more of snow, the trees limned with rime ice.

Bird sounds echo along the road, especially at the lower elevations. Chickadees and titmice chatter as they work from tree to tree, while juncoes flutter among the lower bushes. The hoarse croak of ravens echoes along the entire trail, while the clatter of the pileated woodpecker sounds in the coves.

Animals leave their tracks in the mud and the snow of the road: deer, dogs, foxes, bobcats, and even an occasional bear. The prints of horseshoes left by horses and their riders and the footprints of hikers also show their passing.

The Bald Road passes many beautiful views of the surrounding mountains and the coves that lie beneath. At many places along the road the craggy Eagle Cliffs of the Roan mark the hiker's progress. What seems a world away at the beginning comes closer and closer, until near the end the hiker stares right across to the rock face.

The Bald Road is both a piece of history and a part of the present. Although it was more important in the past for the everyday life of the mountain people, today it serves as a reminder of those times, as well as a pathway to the upper reaches of the mountain.

A battered milk can stands beside the old rock springhouse on the Luther Herrell homeplace.

SPRINGHOUSES

You reach for the dipper
that's gone, then
remember to use your hands
as a cup for the cold
that aches and lingers.

Jeff Daniel Marion

Cold springwater has always been one of the most welcome gifts of the mountains to mankind, as well as to the many animals that have wandered over the slopes and through the valleys. Nothing quenches a thirst better than that simple, sweet liquid.

The Indians and early settlers simply knelt at the springhead to refresh themselves. Later, as farms developed, the

Max Hopson displays his collection of crockware and pitchers.

pure water was captured and funneled to buildings to serve a multitude of purposes.

"The first ones they built they just made a trough with rough boards; later they used pipes," says Max Hopson, principal of Buladean Elementary School and longtime local historian.

During his lifetime Hopson has seen the introduction of electricity and the changes it has brought to many mountain traditions. Gradually, most of the springhouses fell into ruin. However, he has kept his eyes on the ones that have survived and cherishes them as tangible parts of his mountain past.

"There was just one common dipper—a tin dipper that everyone drank from. Or they used a gourd a lot of times as a dipper," he says, remembering the days of his youth and the nail by the door where the dipper hung.

The springhouse was an essential part of the home economy of the region. The icy waters refrigerated as well as refreshed, and they gave a soothing murmur as they flowed through the deep concrete troughs that held them.

"Not that long ago there wasn't any electricity up here. People would bring their butter, milk, and cream to the springhouse to keep them cool and fresh," says Hopson, who remembers well his visits to the springhouse.

In the cash-poor communities of the mountains, using natural resources to create an independent lifestyle became a way of life.

"When I was six years old, we didn't have an electric bill; we didn't have a phone bill. We only bought sugar, coffee, salt, and lamp oil at the store," says Hopson.

The technology of the springhouse was simple, yet effective.

"They used what you call 'crockware.' It kept stuff colder than glass. The crocks didn't have lids. They'd just turn a plate over to cover it," says Hopson, as he brings out several old crocks and pitchers that he has collected over the years.

He points to a large pitcher with a cream-colored base and dark brown collar and spout. It has a sturdy handle for pouring.

"We usually kept sweet milk in that. In that [he points to a smaller brown pitcher with a lid] my mother kept cream or sourdough, so she could make the bread rise. The cream pitcher's probably from the 1800s," says Hopson, kneeling next to the collection.

Oak shingles cover the wood frame springhouse on the old Brad Masters homestead.

"They'd sit right in the spring boxes. They were heavy. They wouldn't float when you got something in them," he says.

In addition to providing free cooling for the housewife, the springhouses also helped to cool extra milk which was sold to bring in scarce dollars and cents.

A battered milk can standing beside an old rock springhouse on the Luther Herrell homeplace is a reminder of an economy that has passed from this place.

"Milk from local farmers was called C-grade milk. They'd cool the milk in the cans in the springhouse until the dairy truck came by," says Hopson, running his hand over the rough rock work of the old building.

"Some like this one they built real fancy, with slats on the end for a breezeway," he says, pointing to the narrow boards that enclose the open end.

Farther up the dirt road that runs by the Herrell farm is the Andrew Byrd homeplace, where a brick building with a tin roof receives the cold springwaters. Hopson guesses it was built in the 1870s, but it looked different then.

Typical of its time, it was a wood frame building with a wood shingle roof; but over the many years it served the Byrd family, it was upgraded to the more durable materials of modern civilization.

Over the hill lies a springhouse that remains as it was first built. A rock foundation supports the wood frame building with oak shingles on the old Brad Masters farm. Hopson's son Dan has bought the farm and hopes to restore the springhouse.

Across the road Gladys Masters is hanging her laundry. Hopson stops to ask her about her springhouse.

"That's where we first got our water, and it kept things just as cool in the summer," says Gladys Masters, as she looks from her neat front yard to her old springhouse sitting in a field.

"But it sure is nice to have it in the house now," she adds.

Max Hopson walks up the roadbed he has studied for many years.

OLD ROAD

The past is a living presence in parts of Southern Appalachia. The land holds the record of former ways of life in the scars on its ancient face. Those who care can read in these signs the story of their forebears.

One such interpreter is Max Hopson, a native of Mitchell County and the principal of Buladean Elementary School. While he is a living link to ways gone by, his keen blue eyes have looked deeply into rutted roadbeds to read even further into his heritage.

For several years he has searched and researched a deeply cut wagon road that runs through his property. The abandoned roadway has brought together different parts of his life as it tells a tale of mountain existence.

"My grandfather had a blacksmith shop. It was right over

there," says Hopson, turning in his chair to point across Highway 226 from his office in the elementary school.

"He made wagon wheels in the '20s. Fidel Birchfield was his name. I helped him when I was five or six year old. I used to turn the forge for him when he was bending iron or something.

"And I got interested in horse-drawn wagons," says Hopson, as he remembers the old days and the man who has slipped into the past.

Studying history at East Tennessee State University kept Hopson's mind running along the same tracks that it had followed when he was a boy. When he returned to Buladean as

Max Hopson displays the wood and iron fragments found in the old road.

The numerals 1888, carved in a beech tree beside the old road, have expanded with the tree over the years.

an educator, he also rediscovered his boyhood interests.

"I got started on horse-drawn wagons and bought some. I did a little research on when they were made and who made them—what companies.

"I've got one made by Montgomery Ward and one made by Studebaker. Studebaker made them in West Bend, Indiana, then changed from wagons to cars and trucks," says Hopson.

One of his favorite manufacturers of wagons was closer to home. The Lamons company in Greeneville, Tennessee, made a variety of wagons and had a good reputation.

"When it went out of business in 1941, Roy Rogers bought the whole factory and moved it to California. I've got three different sizes by Lamons: a log wagon, a farm wagon, and a number three heavy-duty wagon," says Hopson, showing an enthusiasm that goes beyond historical interest.

Collecting the wagons and remembering his blacksmith grandfather led him to the next step—restoring them.

"I've got all the tools for making wagons. I've got the spoke cutters and spoke pullers and all the blacksmith equipment—forge, vices, anvil—everything that they used.

"I've repaired two, even made the axles and wheels and everything," he says.

As he re-created the past with his hands, he also searched into it with his eyes and legs. An old wagon road runs just below his house, which sits on a knoll on the road from Red Hill to Tipton Hill.

Hopson is happy to drive people over to show them the history that runs up the hollow to join the modern hardtop. While most traces of the former road have disappeared under the asphalt of the new one, this one section remains as it was.

"That part of the old road, it's the only section that I know of that wasn't destroyed when the WPA [Work Projects Administration] built the new one back in the late '30s. They built the new road over most of it.

"Here it was saved because they took a different direction off around the hollow, because of the grade, I guess," says Hopson, pointing out the sweeping curves of the new road.

Old-timers in the area told the researcher much about the particular road and also about the ways of travel in the days of wagons.

"A fellow by the name of Lon Tipton knew all about every old wagon road down in this area. He had hauled lumber on wagons for years. He showed me this one and another that goes over to Harrel Hill.

"I guess I was lucky to have two old roads left without much change in them right close to my house," says Hopson.

The historian then moved his research into the field—literally. With a metal detector he probed the roadbed and the surrounding woods and pastures to see what he would find as tangible remains of past ways.

"We hunted it real good, went up and down the road. We found an old revolver—a Colt revolver that had rusted—we plowed it up in that field," he says, pointing to a flat, open pasture above the road.

"In the road we found oxshoes, horseshoes, muleshoes and a ring from an ox yoke. We found part of a wheel that was out here where someone had a breakdown.

"We got the hub, felloes, two or three spokes. The iron rim was gone," says Hobson.

He gets out the remnants, wood and iron fragments of the past. The hub still holds its shape. The felloes, curved pieces of wood that formed the wheel under the iron rim, tell much about its structure. And the various shoes show the kinds of beasts that pulled the loads.

"They would be coming up that hill," he says, pointing to the steep incline where the ruts have dug deep into the soil.

"When you have a load, you pull twenty-five or fifty feet, then stop if it was an uphill grade and let the team rest, then go another twenty-five or fifty feet. That would be steep for a wagon team," he says.

At the base of the incline, a small grove of trees provided shade for resting teamsters. A large beech tree there holds a roughly carved date—1888. The century since it was carved has stretched and expanded the numbers.

"Yeah, that's what happens in a tree. They were probably just about that big when cut," he says, holding his finger a couple of inches apart. The numerals now are over a half foot high and stretch across the curve of the tree.

Looking at the tree and pointing at the date, Hopson's mind runs back over the past century, and farther, travelling the less tangible road of time.

"Probably the first people that settled in this area created the road. It goes back at least to pre-Civil War and went from Red Hill to Tipton Hill. They probably used it for hauling tanning bark over to Toecane.

"It would join up with the old road that went to Johnson City and the old road into Bakersville. Old man Lon said that it was usually a four-day trip to Johnson City, four days and four nights from Red Hill," says Hopson.

Travel was not the only difficult and time-consuming aspect of the old roads. Keeping them open was a community responsibility.

"Before the state formed the Department of Transportation, they would require each adult male to work so many days a year on the roads, repairing the roads.

"They'd fill up mudholes, move boulders that had fallen into the road, haul stone. It was done with pick and shovel and wheelbarrow," says Hopson, pointing to a deeply rutted part of his road where erosion and time have left their marks.

As Hopson walks up the roadbed, his eyes sweep back and forth to find a clue he might have missed over the years. Buladean is fortunate to have a man like Max Hopson to look over the land to read the stories its weathered face tells.

Mr. and Mrs. Frank Mosley

HERBAL TEAS

In the not-so-distant past, when mountain folks invited you to take a cup of tea, they seldom meant Lipton or other orange pekoe teas in a little bag on a string. They offered teas made from roots or leaves gathered from their local environment.

Many folks continue this tradition. Mint tea, catnip tea, pennyroyal tea, sassafras tea, ginseng tea, and other herbal brews refresh and cure what ails you. Gathered in late summer and throughout the fall, the leaves, roots, or bark made part of a mountain dweller's store to get through the winter.

"Peppermint makes good tea," says Frank Mosley, a life-long resident of Buladean "You gather it in late August and hang it up and dry it. Then you put it in a bag to keep the bugs and stuff off."

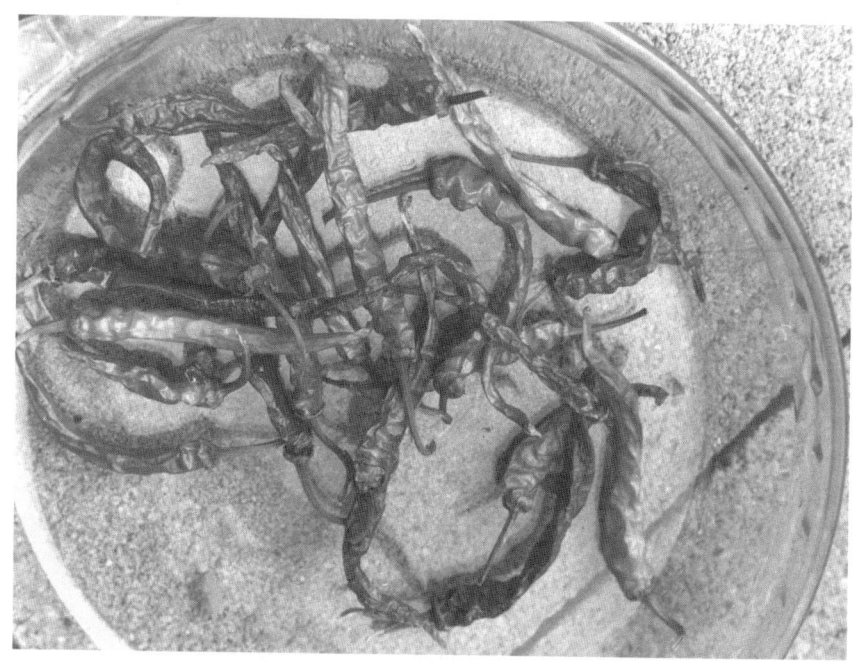

Dried cayenne peppers

He recommends making the tea by steeping the leaves and stalk in hot water, then straining into a cup. He also says peppermint is good to chew, "just like tobacco."

Most folks had patches of the cultivated mint growing around the creeks and other wet places on their property. Peppermint is not so biting as some of the wild mints, which they also gathered.

"We used to go out in the woods and fields and get horsemint, too. We dried it the same way and made tea in the wintertime," says Mosley, sitting comfortably in his easy chair in his wood cookstove-warmed trailer near the fork of Greasy Creek and Rock Creek.

Other mints such as catnip and pennyroyal make excellent beverages, too. In addition to being tasty, soothing hot drinks, the teas also have health benefits.

"That pennyroyal is good for children and babies. It grows in big patches. You just pull it up by the roots and hang it up in bunches and let it dry.

"People doctored with teas when I was growing up. Like pennyroyal, it could cure the bold hives when you made it into tea," says Mosley.

Catnip also soothed and refreshed,

"Catnip—you talk about good tea. Law, you ought to try some. And you talk about making a baby sleep; that catnip tea will do it.

"When Cindy Hopson's little girl was a baby, she had trouble sleeping. We made her some of that tea. She never cried, never even whimpered. She slept just as good," says Mosley, leaning forward to emphasize his point.

While folks used the leaves and stems to make the various mint teas, they sought the roots of other plants to concoct other brews. Sassafras is still a favorite, but in the past it was gathered in much greater quantities by a large number of families.

"About this time of year we'd get it. There used to be a lot of sassafras. You'd get a good-sized tree and cut it off about here, waist high. Then you'd put a chain around it and hook a horse to it and grub it."

Mosley takes his arm to show how the roots of the sassafras tree grow. He holds it straight and crooks his wrist at

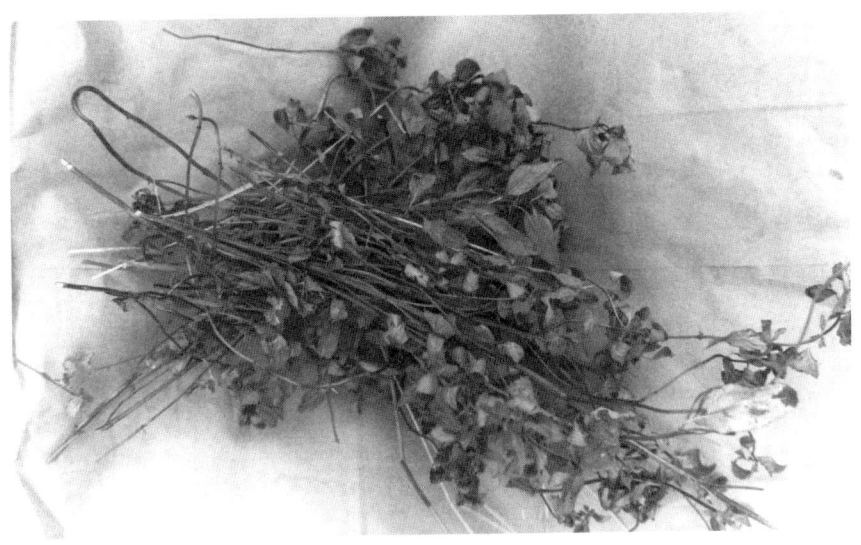

Dried peppermint

a ninety-degree angle to show that one main root runs perpendicular to the trunk.

"Now if you pull away from the root, it'd break right off. You have to pull backwards over the root, and it'll bring a big long root out of there," he says, showing with his hand and arm how the proper pull will work.

Using sleds, Mosley and his neighbors and kin would bring a large load of the sweet-smelling roots down to the settlement. They'd lay the big roots in the branch and wash the mud and soil off them.

"Then we'd skin the bark off the root. It's easy to peel, and it's like an apple; all the flavor is in the peelings. We'd put it in paper bags and dry it. We'd make tea out of it and drink it for supper in the night," he says, smacking his lips.

"The old people, my daddy and mother'd rather have sassafras tea than milk."

Ginseng tea was another root tea that the older generation prized for its healing qualities.

"My daddy'd make tea out of ginseng. He said it was good for rheumatism, what we call arthritis today. He also said that sang tea was the finest thing on earth for the cramp. It'd give you an appetite and make you eat," says Mosley.

Other roots have special virtues, such as butterfly root tea, which was used in the past as a flu treatment. Another cold and flu cure was made from cayenne peppers that had been dried at the end of the growing season by stringing on twine and hanging up.

"You take four or five pods and cut them up with scissors. Put with water in a quart fruit jar with some sugar. Let it sit overnight. You drink a pint jar of it and it'd sweat the flu out. That sheet would be just as wet.

"They'd put a little moonshine liquor in it, and it'd sweat the cold out of you," he says, then smiles at the spicy memory.

Tea in the mountains—it has a whole other meaning than tea in the city.

Frank Mosley kneels to sharpen his knives while he remembers that at age twelve he began learning the skills of hog killing.

HOG KILLING DAYS

Cold days in late fall have their own flavor in the Southern Appalachians. Scattered gunshots can be heard echoing through the wooded coves, mountains stand out clearly in the crisp air, and clouds of steam rise from large vats on crackling fires as families gather for a hog killing.

For generations the ritual was simply another chore come round again to keep everyone fed. For early settlers, the nuts of the forest fattened the wandering hogs that roamed free. Later farmers fed their table scraps to the penned pigs.

The fall slaughter was the same for each as it is today—a hard piece of work that leaves tangible rewards, fat hams salted down for the coming year and fresh tenderloin to fry for dinner.

Mountain folks learned the skills early and refined them

Jerry Putman and others watch as Shorty Mosley scalds the hog.

over the years. Doing it, that's how the Mosleys of Buladean developed their techniques.

"You'll never learn if you won't pick up a knife and start a-learning. Well, I'm seventy-three year old, and I started when I was twelve," says Frank Mosley, as he kneels sharpening a large butcher knife.

He's honed his skills through practice, and seen that his boys have developed theirs, too. Slaughtering hogs for other families was a fall moneymaking enterprise.

"Lord, yeah. I used to kill eighty, me and my boys. Killed eighty-five one year. I started learning my boys when they was six year old. At ten year old they could scrape a hog and cut it up theirselves," says the patriarch, pointing with a knife to three of his now-grown sons working on a large Yorkshire hog.

First, Frank uses a mill file, then a sharpening stone to put a razor edge on the knives. While he works, his sons douse the hog with near-boiling water, then scrape it with the knives to shave off the hair.

"I had eight children, and we had to grow what we eat. I'd kill four to five hogs, a big beef, and about seventy-five chickens each year. We used to kill a hog and have tenderloin for breakfast that morning," says Frank, keeping one eye on his

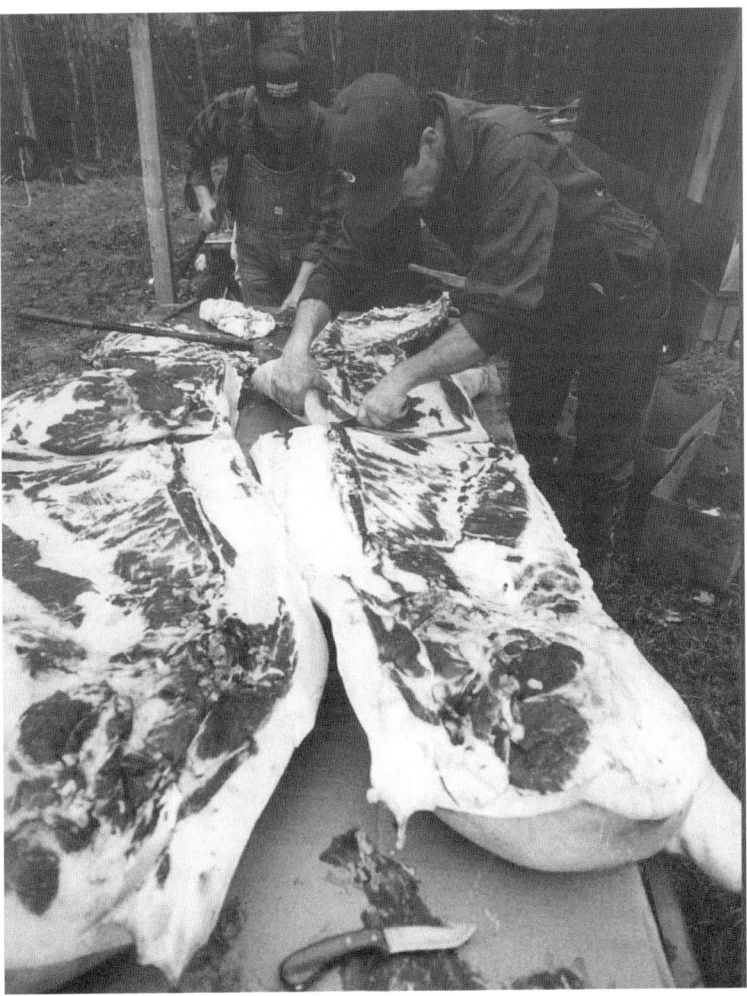

Rob Mosley works with his axe while Shorty Mosley slices with a knife to butcher the hog.

boys as they hang the hog and swiftly work with knife and axe.

"Daddy's supervisor," says his son Rob, working with brothers Larry and Shorty and neighbors Jerry Putman and Norris Davis. Old friend Dallas Street and his son Carroll have journeyed from Pennsylvania to share the work and the memories.

Sister Shelby Jean records the process on her camcorder, recognizing that what was once a simple chore has become an endangered part of their heritage.

Rob Mosley's sons Jason, fourteen, and Cody, eight, are present, but they don't throw themselves into the work. Visits to the grocery store are their assurance that there'll be meat through the winter. Jason observes from the edges, and Cody serves coffee.

"I've done this ever since I was this big," says Rob, holding his hand about mid thigh. "Jason's down here, but he ain't too enthusiastic about it. There's a lot of difference between wanting to and doing it."

"Take note, Jason. Someday Dad will be too old," says Rob's wife, Debby, as Rob uses a short double-bitted axe to chop up the ribs from the hog that now lies on a makeshift table, a large piece of plywood set on pallets.

This is the third hog they've done this morning. By 10:15 this last one is cut up and stored away. Larry's portion fills the back of his pickup truck, and Rob's lies in salt in his curing shed.

"That's what makes it good—salt and brown sugar. For two hogs use about five pounds of brown sugar to twenty-five of salt. If you put too much salt, you get it so salty you can't eat it," says Frank, looking over Rob's work as he packs the salt and sugar around the hams.

The next part of the ritual is the most satisfying—sitting down to a dinner of fresh tenderloin and gravy, creamed corn, mashed potatoes, and biscuits. That fresh flavor is the essence of a cold fall morning in the mountains.

John Tyler

CHRISTMAS PAST

During this century great changes have come to the Southern Appalachians. The folks who grew up during the first three decades of the twentieth century have seen one civilization pass into another.

Today, houses blaze with bright lights and all the other trappings of the Christmas season. Each house has its tree decorated with lights and ornaments. Wreaths and holly and manger scenes are everywhere.

But Christmas in the mountains has not always been celebrated so lavishly. Older mountain folks remember a time gone forever—a simpler, more austere time when Christmas meant an old stocking hung by the roaring fire.

"We didn't know what Christmas was when I was born eighty-six year ago. We'd hang up a stocking, old thick ribbed stockings like we used to make. If we got a piece of candy, we'd be happy," says Pauline Street as she sits in her warm living room on Greasy Creek.

On her sofa stands a large Saint Nick and an oversized white teddy bear dressed in red with a Santa cap. Poinsettias decorate the room, and a small Christmas tree made of flashing lights sits before her window.

"We didn't know what Santa Claus was back then. My mother died when I was five year old, and my grandmother took care of us. Times was hard. Law, law, it was pitiful," says Pauline, remembering the cold winter nights in the cabin, yet the anticipation as stockings were hung around the fireplace.

Pauline Street

Mary Burleson

When Pauline went to an orphanage in Misenheimer, North Carolina, she found a more elaborate celebration.

"We had kind of a celebration. They'd have a play, a savior play, and we'd eat chicken for dinner," says Pauline, her pale blue eyes glistening.

"I got me a job at North American Rayon when I was fifteen. Then I would put me up a tree in Elizabethton when Christmas came," she says, recalling her independence and the joy of the season.

Pauline's neighbor, Mary Burleson, grew up on Greasy Creek. Her family celebrated Christmas in much the same way as Pauline's did.

"We'd put us a stocking up. We'd put it on each side of the fireplace. Papa'd fill it full of candy and put a big orange on top. I wanted a doll so bad. I'd see that orange on top of the stocking and think maybe it was a doll," says Mary, recalling her childhood hopes.

"Papa would always go and buy candy and oranges and raisins. Mom would bake all kinds of cakes and apple pies. There weren't no toys. People didn't take Christmas big like they do now," she says, nodding her head emphatically.

A knocking at the door interrupts her, and she calls, "Come on in!" and in comes John Tyler. He joins the reminiscing.

"Well, it was pretty tough times, but I always got a stick of candy. I'd take my sock and hang it up by the fireplace. In the morning I'd see Santy Claus's tracks where he'd come down the chimney. There'd be a patch of ashes knocked down, and he'd step in it and track around," says John, who grew up in the Great Smoky Mountains.

He remembers one Christmas quite well. He'd begun to have his suspicions about Santa Claus, and he and his brother decided to wait up to see. But they got into mischief with all that waiting.

They went back into the woods where they caught a screech owl. They brought it back to the cabin, where they tied its legs and hid it in their sister's bed.

"Mother said it was about time for Santy Claus to come, 'time for you to go to bed.' We said 'okay' and hung up our socks and away we went. I heard them cracking candy and rattling papers. Sister, she came into bed then.

"She turned over in the bed and musta bumped the owl. It bit her on the leg. She said, 'Whoooeee!' We covered up our heads, but I couldn't keep from laughing. She said, 'Something in my bed! Something in my bed!'" says John, who then chuckles at the memory.

His mother ran in and took his sister into the kitchen. His father jumped up and came running in with a flashlight. When he threw the covers back, the owl flew up into his face.

He cut it loose and turned it outside.

"He shut the door and turned around. He said, 'You boys asleep?' He said, 'I'd whup both of you for doing this here caper, but I can't whup you for having fun on Christmas night. I used to like to have fun myself on Christmas,'" relates John.

He remembers popping popcorn to string for a Christmas tree garland. The popcorn strings and candy canes, "things I called walking sticks," were the only ornaments.

"We never did buy nothing at the store," he says, pushing his cap back on his head.

Warren Campbell agrees. There were no store-bought toys for Christmas.

"Back then they didn't have no toys. We thought there was Santy Claus just like other children till we growed up. We'd hang our socks up around our fireplace. My daddy'd buy apples and oranges and candy. Mother'd bake all kinds of pies and cakes.

"Sometimes my sisters would cut out and make decorations out of paper, make them chains," says Warren, sitting back to catch the sun shining through his workshop window.

His sister Bertie Ledford remembers those days well. She and her sisters created paper chains with colored paper and paste made from flour and water. There were plenty of good things to eat. And Santa Claus would come to visit.

"Whenever we was young our Uncle Jimmy Campbell would put on a false face and a hat. He would come down by the mill house aside the creek. He would take and holler, 'Ho! Ho! Ho!'" says Bertie, who also recalls there were no toys, "not like today."

Despite the simplicity of the past mountain Christmases, most of the older folks agree with Bertie when she says, "We had a good life up in here. We was happy."

The old store sits where the flood left it.

1901 FLOOD REMNANT

A large frame building stands in a rich bottom beside Big Rock Creek between Buladean and Red Hill. The tin-roofed building has a slight list to the rear, but it will last a few more years as a home for cattle and farm implements.

The structure formerly served another purpose. The presence of decorative window frames is one clue that the old gray barn is not what it used to be. Also, it is obvious that a shed has been tacked onto one side where the vertical boards clash with the horizontal ones of the main building.

The memories of old-timers hold the story.

Folks from miles around used to buy their everyday needs here. The building had two stories filled with everything from canned goods to kegged nails. However, at that time, almost a hundred years ago, it stood a couple of hundred yards farther up the creek.

"It was the time of the May Flood. I can't hardly tell you the year. It stood right there below that barn," says Nora Garland, pointing across the driveway to a structure in the pasture on the bank of the creek.

"The flood washed it down there, where it lodged against three big sycamore trees," she says, pointing down where the old building now stands. "And it was full of goods when it washed away."

"My daddy used to work in that store that washed away. He told me all about it," says Nora, looking at the weathered boards that have been a fixture throughout her life.

The flood whose year escapes her memory was the May freshet of 1901. It hit Mitchell County hard, carrying away homes, businesses, and livestock. The flood altered the face of the county for many years.

"All cultivation of the mountainside ceased in 1901 with the coming of what was known to local people as the 'May Flood.' So far as we know, nothing so devastating has ever

Big Rock Creek swept the old store from the barn on the right to its position in the middle of pasture.

Nora Garland

happened in this area before or since," wrote Robert B. Phillips in his memoir, *One of God's Children in the Toe River Valley.*

"Huge pockets of water accumulated and gushed out of the hillside with such fury as to take with them any timber, rocks, or other obstructions in their path. Gulleys were left so deep and wide that cultivating them again was impossible," he added.

Stories of the May Flood have been passed down from generation to generation. Max Hopson, principal of Buladean Elementary School, heard about it from his father, Garrett, who learned about it from his father and mother, A. W. and Lillie Belle Hopson.

"The whole family had to get out of the house and go up on the ridge, the creek rose so high. They left and got out on the little knoll up there in the valley to be safe when it came down," says Max Hopson, remembering his grandfather's stories.

"Lace Parker's store got washed away, I think," he says, then reaches for the phone to call his father. Garrett Hopson fills in the gaps for his son.

Two stores in Buladean were washed away by the flood: one right across from the present elementary school (Max Hopson points to a site across the road) and one up toward the Tennessee line (he points north up the highway). Elisha Street stayed with his store so long that neighbors had to rescue him with a rope.

"When they built the road, they took gravel out of the creek and dug up two kegs of old, rusted nails, cut nails. They bonded together from the rusting. They came from one of those stores," says Max Hopson, the historian of today, meeting the mountain boy of yesterday, in his memories of the find.

But more than nails were lost in the flood.

According to research by Patricia LaBach of Spruce Pine, "All the minutes of the Mitchell County Board of Education prior to May 21, 1901, were lost in the disastrous flood of that date, which swept away twelve houses, a church, and a mill in Bakersville, and left 500-700 persons in Mitchell County without food or clothing."

Harvey Miller in his "News from Pigeon Roost" column wrote, "Several old-timers here said that [the great flood of 1916] was nothing compared to the great May flood."

He reported that one man remembered seeing Aunt Ellen Miller's waterwheel-powered gristmill floating down the creek with "a white cat that acted unconcerned setting on the roof of the building," which stayed together as it floated out into the river.

"He said the cat went on down the Chuckey River," wrote Miller, who added that all the bridges were washed away, and horses and cattle drowned in the flood.

The old-timers who told their tales to Harvey Miller in 1961 have left this earth. The old building that stands almost erect in the Garland bottomlands is one of the survivors that can tell the tale, however silently, of the May Flood of 1901.

Big Rock Creek gurgles by in its bed, seeming to chuckle quietly with its own memories.

Roan Mountain closes horizon on North Carolina side of Iron Mountain Gap.

IRON MOUNTAIN GAP

Regular traffic passes through Iron Mountain Gap day and night throughout the year. On the North Carolina-Tennessee border where Tennessee Highway 107 meets North Carolina Highway 226, Roan Mountain fills the horizon on the North Carolina side and the Appalachian Trail crosses the gap at a crossroads for pedestrians and vehicles.

Few folks who travel through this pass between Mitchell County and Unicoi County know its antiquity. Two hundred years ago the French botanist and explorer Andre Michaux made his way through Iron Mountain Gap. It was a difficult, lonely passage.

In March 1796 Michaux wrote in his journal, "Arrived at Lime Stone cove and slept at Charles Collier's 18 miles from Colonel Tipton's (which was located 10 miles from Jonesborough). The 22nd crossed Iron Mountain and arrived at night at David Becker's, 23 miles without seeing a house."

"David Becker's" was probably David Baker's. Baker lived on the Cane River at the site of today's Bakersville, North Carolina, which was named for him.

Six years later Francois Andre Michaux followed his father's footsteps over the steep path to Iron Mountain Gap. He started his trip

F. A. Michaux crossed the gap in 1802 and described the difficulties.

on horseback from "one Cayerd's at Limestone Cove." He described the commencement and first leg of his journey:

"After having made the most minute inquiry with regard to the path I had to take, I set out about eight o'clock in the morning from Limestone Cove, and after a journey of three hours I reached the summit of the mountain, which I recognized by several trees with 'the road' marked on each, and in the same direction to indicate the line of demarcation that separates the state of Tennessee from that of North Carolina."

The distance from Limestone Cove to the top he found to be two and a half miles, and the distance to the foot of Iron Mountain on the other side in what is today the Buladean community to be three miles.

"The declivity of the two sides is very steep, insomuch that it is with great difficulty a person can sit upon his horse, and that half the time he is obliged to go on foot. Arrived at the bottom of the mountain, I had again, as the evening

Truck goes through Iron Mountain Gap into North Carolina.

before, to cross through forests of rhododendrum, and a large torrent called Rocky Creek, the winding course of which cut the path in twelve or fifteen directions," he wrote.

F. A. Michaux described the difficulties of finding the path when he emerged from the creek at each ford. Today, this rocky "torrent" is known as Big Rock Creek, which collects the waters from the Roan and Iron Mountains to dash down and join the Toe River.

He was happy to reach his goal and considered himself fortunate to have survived.

"I then perceived the imprudence I had committed in having exposed myself without a guide in a road so little frequented, and where a person every moment runs the risk of losing himself on account of the sub-divisions of the road, that ultimately disappear, and which would be impossible to find again," he wrote.

Over the entire twenty-three miles he made his way "without meeting with the least kind of plantation." The country was sparsely settled, indeed.

By the summer of 1854, the road was slightly better marked, as Frederick Law Olmsted found when he traveled from Bakersville to Elizabethton while trying to get to Greensville, Virginia, in the course of gathering material for his book, *A Journey in the Back Country*. Following the mileposts to Bakersville, he went right through the "city," which was made up of three log cabins spaced within a quarter mile of each other.

Feeling uncertain, Olmsted stopped "two great Tennessee bacon wagons" and asked one of the drivers how far it was to Bakersville. When the driver replied that he had never heard of the town and that he had seen no village for twenty miles, Olmsted returned to the houses.

The first was unoccupied, with a stake propped against the door to keep it closed. At the next house he found a man who affirmed that he was indeed at Bakersville, but the man had never heard of Greensville.

"The shortest way into Virginia, he thought, was to cross Iron Mountain into Tennessee. My map (thus agreeing with his advice,) showed a road to Elizabethton, thence a straight road to Greensville. So I followed the road over the mountain, and soon found mile posts reading thus, TOEBIOM (i.e., To Eliza-Bethton, 10 miles)," wrote Olmsted, dating his entry from Elizabethton (pronounced Lizzi Bethton), Tenn., July 15th.

During the Civil War, the Union sympathizers massacred by Confederate raiders at Limestone Cove had crossed Iron Mountain Gap shortly before they were attacked in the cove.

The gap crossed by the two Michauxes, Olmsted, and the Union supporters was slightly north of today's pass, which was carved out to accommodate wheeled vehicles—initially horse-drawn wagons. Many older residents of Buladean remember taking wagons over Iron Mountain Gap to peddle produce in Johnson City.

Both Garrett Hopson and his wife, Stella, first made the trip as children with their fathers over seventy years ago.

"It was a little ol' wagon road," says Stella, recalling the adventure of those days. "I remember I went with my daddy and my sister Cordelia on a wagon peddlin' one time. We was two days a-going to Johnson City with a load of apples."

"It was a three day trip, says Garret, rubbing his chin as he looks back over the years. "Go one day and get down there. Then next day you'd have to sell out. Next day, come back. We took apples, taters, and beans, a bit of everything."

"The road was narrow. Some places were so narrow nobody could pass," says Stella, nodding her head.

Portions of the old trail can be found along the highways on either side of the gap. These narrow, hard-packed strips still carry traffic, but now it is deer and foxes rather than men, women, and horses. On the Appalachian Trail just north of today's gap, the old intersection can easily be found with its trails deeply worn into the soil.

Rock Creek continues to flow down the slopes in a torrent, its rocky bed a challenge to cross. Both trail and creek tell of the past, speaking in faint whispers that must be carefully pursued.

Milan (left) and Marshall stand in front of their sawmill.

MARSHALL STREET'S SAWMILL

The powerful throb of the large diesel engine keeps the fifty-six-inch circular saw humming, until the carrier brings a two-foot-thick log into contact with the sharp teeth. Then the hum disappears under the shriek of the saw's biting through the pine log.

The carrier slides back, and a toothed post pops up to it to turn the log onto its other side. The teeth automatically adjust the log to the proper position for sawing, then the carrier slides forward again, and the shrieking saw spits pine dust.

Milan Street sits in a glass booth with his hands on two control boxes. His fingers press stainless steel buttons, and his feet work pedals to control the machinery while he sits comfortably in a contoured seat.

Just a few months ago he was standing by the carrier, jerking the logs around with a stout peavey while his father, Marshall, worked to adjust the far end, before sending the logs into the teeth of the saw. The sawyer's job was hard manual labor.

Change has been gradual but constant during the time that four generations of Streets have run a sawmill on the banks of Big Rock Creek in Buladean. But despite the innovations, sawmilling for Milan is not that different than it was for his great-granddaddy Brown Street.

Some of the work is easier, but the open-air independence and steady commitment to day in, day out labor remains the same.

As in the past, the Streets and their workers spend dry weather days out in the woods cutting timber and rainy or snowy days at the sawmill. Their work begins at daybreak, just as it did in earlier times.

"We logged with horses up until the 1970s, then we started logging with a bulldozer. We used to load logs with peaveys by hand; now we use a forklift," says Marshall Street, pausing from his work of driving the forklift used to move logs down to the carrier.

He points to the business end of his sawmill.

"That new mill, it's a lot easier on the sawyer and does away with the man back there, and it's a lot faster. Milan's the sawyer now," he says, a note of pride in his quiet voice.

Milan sits confidently in his booth, introducing logs to the saw and watching the large tree boles turn into stacks of fresh boards. He is part of a tradition that is reflected in the equipment around him.

The diesel engine that drives the saw is over thirty years old. His granddaddy was the sawyer then.

"That motor, my daddy bought it in '57. We run it thirty year, then had it rebuilt. Back in the early '50s they sawed with a steam engine. My daddy was the first brought a diesel motor in here," says Marshall, as he sits on a large poplar log during a break.

Milan climbs from his booth to drive a truckload of pine

slabs to the lot next door for dumping. Not many people want green pine slabs, so they'll let them dry out in the lot. This time of year, poplar and hardwood slabs are in demand for firewood. Folks want more truckloads than Milan can deliver.

The Streets have five straight trucks, two bulldozers, and three forklifts. "Then we use the farm tractor a little, you know," says Marshall.

The Streets and their workers handle all maintenance themselves, being almost as good mechanics as they are sawyers. Marshall shakes his head modestly.

"Well, Ben Barlow, now he's a good mechanic," says Marshall, pointing to a bearded man in a blue plaid shirt. He runs the rough boards through a machine that trims the sides.

Milan returns the truck to its position at the end of the mill, where a conveyor system dumps the rough slabs. The

Milan Street operates the new mill from a glass booth as the 56-inch blade bites into a log.

new mill goes back into operation as he climbs back into his high-tech booth.

Marshall loads more logs with the forklift onto the platform. The machinery automatically feeds them to the carrier, where Milan directs the equipment to set them up for sawing, then pushes them into the blade.

At 2:30 in the afternoon the men quit work. As the diesel engine stops, the saw comes to rest. Silence settles over the sawmill. The gurgling creek can be heard for the first time since the engine cranked up early in the morning.

Milan comes to stand by his father.

"Milan's the sawyer, and he's the fourth generation," says Marshall, nodding towards his son, who shyly ducks his head.

"Well, I'm *not* the sawyer . . .," Milan begins, reluctant to assume his father's position. They argue quietly for a minute, reaching a compromise understanding.

"It didn't take him long at all to learn how to run the new mill," says Marshall.

"It was easy to get used to. It's all hydraulics and electric; that other one was manual," says Milan, minimizing his accomplishment.

They both admit the work is easier, at least the sawyer's job. The sweat and danger in the woods is about what it was, although Marshall misses the horses.

"I liked it. I still keep horses, but I don't log them now," he says, then tells Milan to drain the pumps before leaving.

They'll be back tomorrow, continuing the family tradition of hard work and independence.

The orchard sells apples, as well as apples-in-a-bottle.

ORCHARD AT ALTAPASS

Apples and apple orchards have always been a distinctive part of our American heritage, as American as—well—apple pie and Johnny Appleseed. For generations, the Blue Ridge has been regarded as a particularly productive place for growing the versatile fruit, with many orchards thriving on the rich, temperate slopes.

Between Gillespie Gap and McKinney Gap on the Blue Ridge Parkway lies a venerable orchard established in the first decade of this century, but also with a rich earlier history. The Overmountain Men traveled the old road that runs through the trees, and area patriarch Charles McKinney had maintained his four wives and forty-eight children on its rich soil.

For years the orchard provided work and sustenance for

Orchard at Altapass lies on slopes beneath the Blue Ridge Parkway.

local families, as well as faraway consumers; then in the early 1990s it was abandoned and put on the real estate market, a prime piece for developers. One Florida developer had preliminary plans for building 140 houses on the beautiful slopes just below the Parkway.

Fortunately, an advertisement for the property caught the eyes of Kit Carson Trubey, her brother Bill Carson, and his wife Judy. For years the old orchard had been an important part of their attachment to the mountains.

"From the time I was a teenager we came up to visit our aunt and uncle at Little Switzerland. We came up to pick apples here every fall and to take pictures of the blossoms in the spring," says Trubey, as she sits in the apple-packing house in the midst of the trees heavy with fruit.

The immediate response of the trio was that the orchard was invaluable, a part of the history of the area and of their particular family heritage. They also knew its development potential.

"We felt like we wanted to buy it and to help preserve the integrity of the land and of the Parkway—sort of our gift to God. We wanted very much to see it remain an apple orchard," says Trubey, a realtor from the Raleigh area of North Carolina.

So in January 1995 she purchased the land. Initially, her plan was just to leave it alone, but she quickly recognized that such neglect would mean the end of the orchard's productive life.

"We realized that the orchard has been here for a hundred years, and if we could maintain it, it would be that much better," she says, cutting a slice from one of her apples.

Knowing that the orchard contained many old varieties of apples that are no longer grown commercially, the new owner strongly desired to keep it in a thriving condition. Apples such as the King Luscious, Virginia Beauty, Stayman Winesap, and Early Harvest are available from few, if any, commercial orchards.

With her real estate business keeping her tied down in the Piedmont, she turned to her brother and his wife. Recently retired from IBM, Bill Carson readily agreed to take charge of the new venture, but their initial enthusiasm quickly changed to a realization of how difficult the task would be.

"If we had known how much work it was, we wouldn't have started. Running an orchard is a year-round operation. Spring, summer, and fall are incredibly busy, and last winter we worked every day when the weather would allow it," says Bill, pausing from his work in the packinghouse bustling with visitors.

The partners knew that the orchard could not survive as a viable business if they had to compete on the wholesale apple market. The old trees, many planted in the early years of the century, made the job too labor intensive, so they decided to diversify, to make the orchard itself their product.

They became the Orchard at Altapass, selling their apples and much more. The packinghouse became a gift shop, crafts shop, snack bar, and music hall, as well as retaining its original function for sorting and packing the apples.

"We'll never be a wholesale orchard. We will be a retail orchard. The apple will always be our theme, but we are more than apples. We sell crafts, apple products, and other foods and snacks; and every weekend we have music and hayrides," says Bill as he prepares to welcome a group of tourists who are anxious to hear him tell stories of the area's rich heritage, another attraction of the Orchard at Altapass.

Running a business along the Parkway has its advantages and disadvantages. While a lot of potential customers pass by on the scenic highway, the owners maintain a low profile for the attraction to avoid spoiling the very beauty they seek to preserve.

"We don't want billboards. We need to strike a delicate balance between having people recognize we exist without compromising our integrity," says Kit Trubey, who has already refused several offers of more high profile development.

The Orchard at Altapass is open to visitors from Memorial Day weekend until late fall, whenever winter sets in. It is located at milepost 328.4 on the Blue Ridge Parkway. For information about the Orchard, call 704-765-9531.

L-R: Kit Carson Trubey, Bill Carson, Judy Carson

*Visitors videotape Cool Springs Baptist Church and informa-
tion sign.*

JEFFRESS PARK

The story of early mountain settlers, picnic sites, hiking
trails, natural history, scenic beauty, and cooling cascades
are all part of the Blue Ridge Parkway. At E. B. Jeffress Park
between Boone and West Jefferson, you can enjoy all of these
attractions at one location.

Many travelers on the scenic highway pull off to investi-
gate the two log structures that stand on the eastern side of
the road. Classic mountain log buildings, one was Jesse
Brown's cabin and the other was the meeting house of the
Cool Springs Baptist Church.

Roofed with white oak shingles rived the old-fashioned
way, the weathered log shelters have dovetailed corners, door
frames joined to the logs with wooden pegs, and rock foun-
dations. The hewing marks show clearly on the sides of the

squared logs. A solidly set stone chimney is joined to the Brown cabin.

A sign next to the simpler building explains that it served primarily as Cool Springs Baptist Church's shelter from the weather, because circuit riding preachers Willie Lee and Bill Church would hold their services outdoors. Inside the unchinked building a small field mouse is the only permanent church member today, but many visitors stop by to read the sign and to take pictures of the rough structure.

The travelling preachers would spend the night in Jesse Brown's cabin, according to the sign, "before travelling on to other soul-saving appointments." Most visitors stroll between the two buildings, effortlessly learning a simple lesson about early mountain ways of life.

Apple trees loaded with ripening fruit continue to provide their bounty, even though the farm itself holds no family to gather and store the gold and red globes in late summer and early fall.

Notched logs dovetail at corners of Cool Springs Baptist Church building.

Below Brown's cabin, just under the edge of the woods, lies a small springhouse, with cool water still carried by hollowed logs from the springhead. One log brings the water to the springhouse, then another carries it through, while also serving as trough for milk or butter vessels.

The cold water

then pours from the log to flow through the woods. This place provides a cool respite on hot summer days. The sound of the gurgling water, the breeze through the trees, and the chirping birds invite you to rest a while.

And many visitors are ready for a cooling rest, for they arrive at the cabin clearing from hiking trails that run throughout Jeffress Park. The parking lot is several hundred yards north of the cabins where there are bathrooms and picnic tables.

Some travelers simply stop for the convenience and comfort of these facilities. Some picnic tables overlook the valley and distant foothills to the east of the Blue Ridge. Large oaks and other hardwoods provide shade for diners.

Hiking trails begin from this area. The Cascades Trail takes you through the forest where Falls Creek flows, then down to rocky balconies that overlook the startlingly beautiful cascades. Plaques erected along the trail provide an education on the natural history of the region and tie the forest to the lives of the settlers.

Under a black locust tree you are told that "according to a certain farmer, 'A post of locust will outlast rock 2 to 1. I know because I tried it twice.'" At a black gum tree, you read that twigs from this species are used as "chaw sticks" by mountain folks to place snuff behind their lips.

The name of the doghobble bush is explained. "A bear dog on a hunt, loping along with his nose to the ground, has often plunged unseeing into a leucothoe thicket. There, 'hobbled' by the vine, he suddenly finds himself at the mercy of the bear," says the plaque.

You can learn about the pignut hickory, scarlet oak, red maple, black oak, eastern hemlock, witch hazel, birches, rosebay rhododendron, and many other trees and bushes along the trail.

At the bottom of the trail you reach the cascades, where an upper and a lower balcony put you directly beside the white veils of rushing water. A constant breeze rises from the chilly chasm below, as you wonder at the beauty of the falls and gaze at distant farms and hills through the trees.

A plaque at the head of the cascades includes a map and tells the story of Falls Creek's trip down the mountain to join the Yadkin River, then the Pee Dee in South Carolina, before flowing into the Atlantic Ocean at Winyah Bay.

While the return hike from the cascades requires some effort, frequent informative plaques give you a good excuse to stop to rest and read on your way back to the parking lot.

Before leaving, stop to read the sign explaining the origin of the six-hundred-acre park and its dedication to E. B. Jeffress, a North Carolina newspaper publisher who played a role in establishing the Blue Ridge Parkway. To explore everything offered by the park, plan to spend a day on the parkway at milepost 272, just north of Deep Gap.

Blanche Joslin enjoys the falls from the lower overlook.

The cemetery at Presbyterian Church holds remains of many early Banner Elk families.

BANNER ELK

Nestled protectively between Beech Mountain and Sugar Mountain lies the small town of Banner Elk. Today a popular resort area, much of its past has been effaced by development, yet traces can be found to reveal its history, as well as voices to tell its story.

"If sympathy is sorrow, then I am acquainted with grief, grief for the pioneer fathers and mothers of Banner Elk who earned their beautiful valley so hard and are now remembered so poorly," wrote Shepherd Monroe Dugger early in this century, when a surge of progress came to his village.

Even at that time the past seemed to be in danger of being swallowed up by the present. Dugger and some of his contemporaries tried to keep alive the community's heritage.

The first settler in the Banner Elk area arrived during the

Revolutionary War. Samuel Hix, who sought security in the wilderness, either to avoid forced military service or to flee those angered by his Tory activities, became an outlier in the area where the Grandfather Home for Children is now located.

Hunting, fishing, and gathering from the abundant resources of the virgin forest, and farming the rich land, Hix established himself for a number of years. The "Hix Improvement" became a well-known feature of the frontier and attracted a Welshman, John Ollis, who made his own rough encampment nearby.

The first permanent settlers of the area were fugitive lovers seeking to establish a life for themselves. John Holtsclaw, a married church deacon with seven children, eloped in 1825 with the teenaged Delilah Baird from her home in Valle Crucis.

Telling her that he had a home for her in Kentucky, Holtsclaw carried her on a circuitous route into Tennessee along the Doe and Elk rivers, back into North Carolina to his lean-to on the Elk River near the present site of Banner Elk. Thinking she was in far-off Kentucky, Delilah settled into the wilderness life with her man on his grant of 480 acres.

The forest and river provided abundantly for the couple. Deer provided meat and skins; bears also gave rich food and warm fur. The river yielded trout, and the woods a large variety of herbs. In the fall, Delilah wandered far into the mountains gathering ginseng.

Although wild animals such as panthers, bears, bobcats, and wolves roamed the forest, she had little fear. One day, as she reached the crest of a mountain, she heard a cowbell clanging nearby. The bell made a sound just like the bell on her father's cow, Sooky.

Investigating, she found that it was the very same cow and bell. Her lover had tricked her. Instead of going to Kentucky, they had moved only eight miles away. But she readily forgave her man when she returned home.

"I want to thank you for taking me off and making me

From Lees-McRae College campus, Beech Mountain can be seen overlooking Banner Elk.

think I was in Kentucky. It don't matter that this ain't Kentucky. I couldn't have been no happier," she said, nestled in his arms.

Soon the couple had a baby. Alfred B. Baird, born March 7, 1826, was the first child born in what was to become Banner Elk. The family grew over the years. Delilah died in 1890 and is buried in the Baird Cemetery in Valle Crucis.

The Banners, who gave the town its name, arrived in the 1840s. Martin Banner came first, followed by his five brothers, who began to carve a productive life from the wilderness.

"It was first called Banner's Elk, for the Banners' place on the Elk River. There were a lot of elk there too," says Charles Von Canon, a descendant of the Banners and William Von Canon, his grandfather, the son of Jacob Von Canon, who arrived shortly after the Banners.

"They built cabins in the deep solitudes where bears and wolves, wildcats, and panthers skulked in the woods, and great eagles swept through the sky like wind-clouds. The rifle, the axe, and the trap were their implements of support," wrote Shepherd M. Dugger, whose ancestor G. W. Dugger was another early settler along with Levy Moody and Joel Eggers.

"I used to enjoy sitting in my grandfather's home in front of his fireplace hearing his stories of hunting elk and other animals," says Charles Von Canon, who at eighty-two years of age is a direct link to the founding fathers and mothers of the town of Banner Elk, for his grandfather married a Banner.

The Civil War disturbed the tranquil life of the settlers. Like many areas of the mountains, Union sympathy was great, although there were some who supported the Confederacy. William Von Canon and several others supported the Union cause, while Frank Banner enlisted in the Southern army.

"They had a tradition in this community. Each side took care of the other side. When my grandfather got wounded, the Banners took care of him until he got to where he could work his farm again," says Von Canon, remembering the stories told to him.

Banner's Elk was established as a post office in Watauga County on June 16, 1875. Martha Banner was named postmaster and served until 1885. The name of the post office was not changed to Banner Elk until May 1, 1937.

A budding tourism industry began to thrive about this time. Dugger wrote that "boarders were Professor Car, our State Geologist, and his family; then came the Rankin ladies of Lenoir, who from a point in Dr. Banner's meadow made a superb oil painting of Beech Mountain. Then fishermen came from Chattanooga, Tenn., including Zen Wheeler, T. H. Payne and gentlemen of the Chattanooga Medicine Co."

The Klonteska Inn and Banner Elk Hotel flourished, hosting guests from May through the fall. Most of the visitors stayed for several months, enjoying the cool weather and the bountiful meals. Today, the Banner Elk Hotel still stands, as the home of Charles Lowe, the last of his line, who no longer takes guests but lives with his memories.

In late 1895, Edgar Tufts, a seminary student, arrived in the town to perform summer service for the Presbyterian Church. He was destined to have a great impact on Banner Elk. After he was ordained, he returned and over the years established a school which eventually became Lees-McRae College, a hospital which is today Cannon Memorial Hospital, and an orphanage which is now Grandfather Home for Children.

In 1911, Banner's Elk was chartered as the town of Banner Elk. Minutes of the first meeting of the officers appointed by the North Carolina General Assembly show that L. D. Lowe was mayor; Rev. Edgar Tufts, R. L. Lowe, and F. H. Stinson were commissioners; and J. H. Von Canon was town marshall.

When Avery County was formed later that year, Banner Elk became part of that county. Surviving minutes reveal that town officers were concerned with such things as cattle wandering freely in the streets, drunk and disorderly citizens, the discharge of fireworks, and logs and other heavy objects being dragged along the streets. Ordinances were passed to prevent all of these abuses.

In 1932, Banner Elk was recognized as an ideal place to live. "Recently the Associated Press sent nationwide the news that Banner Elk, N.C., was the 'perfect town' for 1932. There had not been need to spend a cent for relief, there had been no business failure or foreclosure, no one had been arrested, there was money in the town treasury, and taxes had been lowered from 40 cents to ten cents, and not a bootlegger had been caught," wrote *The State*, a Columbia, S.C., newspaper, in a feature article that examined the success of the town.

Rev. Tufts's son, Edgar H. Tufts, president of Lees-McRae College, responded to questions of the newspaper by explaining how all of this was possible. He ended with this paragraph:

"My personal opinion is that the people of Banner Elk, far from being illiterate and yet by no means sophisticated, have shown themselves in one way to be better educated then residents of many larger towns. They have never been led by the sound of the word 'Progress' without stopping to inquire just what 'Progress' means. The word implies not only motion, but motion with a definite purpose. Banner Elk has the ingrained habit of inquiring into purpose before entering into motion. As a result, today it is still a small village, but a happy and contented one."

Unfortunately, things have changed in the town since that time. Outside developers have often acted without considering what "progress" will mean to the community in the long run. Too often they used the traditional independence of the mountain people as a method of forestalling regulations.

"When I was mayor, we decided that we needed some kind of control. Development was happening too fast. We started working on zoning and land use restrictions," says Charles Von Canon, who served as mayor or county commissioner for twenty-seven years.

"Charles lost his best friend over zoning," says Aileen Von Canon, his wife of sixty years. "He was our best man at our wedding. We got threatening phone calls; it was frightening."

"The first thing they said was, 'This is my land, and I will do whatever I want with it.' We did get some zoning and land use controls, but it's awfully hard. It's just fighting all the time," says Von Canon, looking out his window where a backhoe is removing tons of silt which choked off the creek running by his house and also filled in the old millpond that for years provided hydroelectric power to the town.

In the past few years, flooding and silting of creeks and rivers has become a major problem for the town, a problem which arrived with the developers and has no easy solution.

"Back years ago they didn't farm any land that was too steep. They grew trees on it, and none of the land washed away. Today, we can't control development outside the city, but the erosion and floods come down on us," says Von Canon, who continues to work to preserve the mountain environment that he loves.

Stylish boutiques, expensive restaurants, and high-class

antique stores have recently found a place in downtown Banner Elk, serving the tourists and vacation home owners who flock to the area to enjoy the cool summer weather, the beautiful fall foliage, and the winter ski season.

Land that displays a rural character is being sold for commercial development that increases the pressure on the environment and on the old ways of life. The simplicity of the past is threatened, but knowledge of what was good can perhaps help prevent what may be lost.

"We love the mountains, and protecting the environment will preserve that life. Also, if we destroy what we have, we will destroy the tourists that it brings to us," says Charles Von Canon, whose memories help fuel his enthusiasm for the task.

Edgar Tufts and his wife, Mary Elizabeth Tufts are shown with their children, Margaret, in front, and Edgar Hall, in back.

EDGAR TUFTS

One hundred years ago a young, newly ordained Presbyterian minister came to the mountains of Western North Carolina as an evangelist. His ministry has changed forever the community of Banner Elk as well as surrounding areas he touched.

While Edgar Tufts was sent to care for the souls of the people, he dedicated his life to ministering to their physical and mental needs, as well as their spiritual ones. He left an enduring legacy in the shape of churches, a school, a hospital, and a children's home that have become important institutions evolving with the times.

He also left to us a model of Christian service and stewardship that is more difficult to document but must not be forgotten. His daughter Margaret Tufts Neal, in her 90s, remembers well her father's simple creed.

"He didn't come up here with the plan, 'I'm going to found a school,' or 'I'm going to found a hospital.' It was a matter of answering a need, whether it was a physical need or a spiritual need. That's the idea behind the institutions," she says, sitting in her wheelchair pulled up to a table where her Bible and other books lie.

Miss Margaret, as she is known to generations of Lees-McRae College students and members of the Banner Elk community, has seen and participated in the growth of the institutions founded by her father. The college, Cannon Memorial Hospital, and Grandfather Home for Children are now multi-million dollar establishments with lives of their own.

Several Presbyterian churches for miles around can trace their roots to the ministry of Edgar Tufts. The rock-walled Banner Elk Presbyterian Church overlooks the campus of Lees-McRae College and the town of Banner Elk. Edgar Tufts's grave lies in the shadow of the church he built.

Banner Elk Presbyterian Church was built under Rev. Edgar Tufts's guidance.

Tufts first visited Banner Elk in May 1895. Sent for summer evangelistic work as a student from the seminary in Hampden-Sydney, Virginia, he was not prepared for the weather of the mountains. In an interview in the early 1970s, Anna Guignard recounted his arrival:

"I was the very first one to meet Mr. Tufts. It was in May and snowing, and Mr. Tufts has on a Palm Beach hat and a Palm Beach suit. He was standing there shivering. He said, 'Let me get to a fire.'"

The seminarian started work on the church, then returned the following year to complete the wooden structure that preceded the rock one. Tufts provided more than direction; he threw himself into every aspect of the work. He learned as he went, enjoying the adventure of the task. In a letter to his future wife he wrote:

"You ought to have seen me driving some oxen not long since. I went with a little boy to the mill to get a load of lumber. He knew a little about managing the oxen, and if it hadn't been for him I don't know what would have become of me.

"We didn't have any lines, and when they started down the steep road in a trot, I saw there was no way of stopping them and as there was a high embankment on one side I jumped out. The boy stayed on the wagon, beating and hollering at the oxen as loud as he could. Finally they got to the bottom of the hill and went on all right."

In 1898 he brought his young wife Mary Elizabeth Hall, known as Miss Bessie, to join him in his work at Banner Elk and to live in the house he was building for her.

In 1899 Tufts started a fire-side school that has evolved into Lees-McRae College. Its growth and development are typical of how his simple response to a need flourished far beyond his initial intentions.

"He decided that he would like to have a class. I was one of the chosen ones. We met in Mr. Tufts's home in an upstairs room. We used that one room upstairs to learn Bible, ancient history, mythology, English literature, and mental arithmetic—that I couldn't manage," said Anna Guignard.

The Black Mountains wear a coat of rime ice.

The Black Mountains rise above the clouds on the horizon as snow covers Round Bald.

Catawba Rhododedron blossoms glow in an opening by Upper Creek Falls.

Sun breaks through winter clouds striking snow-covered mountains in the Toe River Valley.

Mint grows next to the worn walls and rock chimney of an old mountain cabin.

A few steps from the old Bald Road, beauty stretches to the horizon across the Toe River Valley.

Morning Glories clothe an old locust fence near Hughes Gap.

An idle disc harrow rests on a mountain farm on Greasy Creek.

A pasture, tobacco field, and woods form a spring mosaic on Howard Burleson's farm.

Del Bachert encourages his suffolk gelding, Ben, to pull.

Bakersville, North Carolina, nestles in the valley under Roan Mountain.

Fall colors and gray rocks create a beautiful scene off the Blue Ridge Parkway.

Tobacco cures in a Virginia Creeper-covered barn on Big Rock Creek.

Fall color defines mountain ridges.

Fall colors glow, accenting the stark beauty of a dead spruce.

Clouds and color bring beauty to the Elk River Valleys.

Miss Margaret explains how from this simple beginning, Lees-McRae grew into the college it is today.

"The school began because they were coming to him to learn. They were already coming on horseback to his house to learn, and the other churches he served had young people who wanted to learn too. They began to ask if they could come and live, either with us or wherever they could find a house," she says, sitting in the same house her father built and that was the site of his first "school."

Margaret Tufts Neal

Tufts decided to built a boarding school to answer this need. He first approached the local people, then the congregations of his various churches to get support for the project. After receiving official approval from the Presbytery, he raised money and accepted contributions of land, lumber, and labor.

In September 1900 he opened the school. He named it the Elizabeth McRae Institute in honor of a respected teacher and church woman, Mrs. McRae from Maxton, North Carolina. In 1903 the name of Mrs. Lees of New York was added in honor of her monetary support. The Lees-McRae Institute has grown to become Lees-McRae College.

Similarly, Cannon Memorial Hospital has grown from a doctor who treated people at his residence established by Tufts, and Grandfather Home from the orphanage Tufts created to care for children who had lost their parents or whose parents could not care for them.

From the beginning Edgar Tufts thought in terms of the individual needs of the people. These needs ranged from the general to the particular. One need that he addressed was to show his mountain people the worth of their way of life and the beauty of their environment.

"He used to say that the native people often didn't appreciate the world around them, much like the people in New England where Thoreau lived didn't. Like Thoreau in Walden, he thought that part of education should be teaching them to appreciate what they had here and to take care of the environment—what is given us," says Miss Margaret, looking out her windows where bluets dot her yard and hundred-year-old hemlocks provide shade.

She then gives an example of his answering a particular need:

"Upstairs are some hand-woven coverlets. There's one we always called 'the Methodist preacher's coverlet.' My father was visiting a family in which the husband had died in the little hospital here. My father stopped to see how they were getting along.

"The mother said they were all right. The boys could do the gardening to raise food. But she was upset because there was no money to give the Methodist preacher at the church. Always before they had given $15 for the session. Father said, 'I will pay you the worth of this spread, and you will have the money to pay your preacher.'

"He brought the spread back here for us to use and left her the money so she could pass it on to the Methodist preacher," says Miss Margaret.

Similarly, Tufts and his institutions accepted produce for tuition or doctor's fees or any other service.

"We had a store down the hill from the church called the Exchange. It meant that men paid their debts with the school with produce they raised, and the same for the hospital and the same with the children's home," says Miss Margaret.

On the wall near her table hangs a faded photograph of Edgar Tufts working at his desk. He looks tired as he pores over his accounts.

"He was losing his hair, not from age, but just as he said, he was 'full of days.' I know it was taken here. I recognize the homemade mailboxes and the lamp I still use," she says, flipping through her Bible to read where David was "full of days."

Edgar Tufts died young. He was only fifty-two years old when he caught pneumonia while riding his horse through the snowy mountains to visit four elderly women who lived alone at the base of Grandfather Mountain. As he lay dying, his son Edgar came with the message that the bell had just been installed in the tower of the rock church.

The women of Banner Elk wove a blanket of galax leaves to line his grave. While a particular stone has his name carved in it above his remains, the true monument to his work continues to grow and evolve—churches, a school, a hospital, a children's home, and the legacy of caring that endures today.

Dogs are the only ones relaxing on the porch of Banner Elk Hotel today.

BANNER ELK HOTEL

The faded paint is an indeterminate color—grey or green or off-white—the roofline sags, and the porches and floors slope this way and that. Yet the old Banner Elk Hotel remains one of the most imposing buildings in this small town at the base of Beech Mountain.

The hotel is a large time capsule, containing pieces of the past preserved into the present. A way of life that has faded and changed as much as the building itself can still be found in the hotel, locked in an old man's memory.

The locked rooms with their old pieces of well-worn furniture tell a quiet tale, but a more brilliant narrative comes from a survivor of that past. Charles Lowe sits in his chair at the center of the former dining room, ready to tell what he remembers of the glory days of his family's hotel.

"Everybody says—older people than I am say—it's 150 years old. Nobody can tell now, but it's been here a long time," says the eighty-five-year-old Lowe, as he shifts to get more comfortable among the cushions padding his chair.

In *The History and Genealogy of Henry Banner and his Descendants 1723-1979*, William Perry Banner wrote that the hotel was established by the Banners before the Civil War and that it was bought in the early 1890s by Charles's parents, Robert Lee and Blanche Von Canon Lowe. The Lowes expanded the building and spent the rest of their lives as host and hostess of the well-known mountain hostelry, raising their family of eight children while building a reputation for bountiful hospitality.

Their son Charles has been part of the hotel his entire life. He saw the hustle and bustle when the hotel's many rooms were full from April to October each year. He helped his sister Fannie run it after their parents died in 1948. And he continues to live among the relics of the past, guarding the hotel from those who want to take parts of it away.

"I've always lived here. Two ladies staying at Beech came

Charles Lowe does chores around the old hotel today just as he did when it was a thriving business.

Charles Lowe stands beneath heavily laden grapevines grow-ing on the old building.

down here and said that they'd heard I had antiques and wanted to see them. I said there wasn't but one in the house and that they were looking right at it," says Charles Lowe, his big grin lighting up the darkened room. "Their faces turned red as a beet.

"People who came here to stay was awful nice. They'd bring their whole family and stay from April or May till October. They knew what it was and liked it," he says, leafing through some old photographs to find one that shows some of the guests gathered on the steps.

The hotel had twenty rooms to rent, parlors, a large dining room and kitchen, and long porches for rocking and watching the shadows play across the face of Beech Mountain, and seeing the seasons pass from the flowers of spring, to the deep green of summer, and to the colorful glory of the mountain fall. The natural attractions of the Elk River Valley drew visitors from all over.

"We called them boarders, not guests. They came from everywhere. We had one family that came from England every summer for twenty years. We had people from Florida to California," says Charles, remembering through the silence of today to a time when the hardwood floors and the cherry-bannistered stairs echoed to the tread of many feet.

Dancing feet also left their marks on the old floor. Today, the dining room floor slopes away from its center, but in the past it supported many a tromping, shuffling pair. The hotel was the center of social life for the area.

In 1975, Anna Belle Von Canon Guignard remembered the early days of the century. Born in 1882, she spent most of her life in Banner Elk.

"We'd meet at the Banner Elk Hotel, that's one of the oldest buildings left. My sister had married and moved there and had summer guests, and we would have a dance every night except Sunday.

"I don't know what we did on Sunday, I guess we tried to be good," she told an interviewer.

Charles Lowe also remembers well the dances.

"Oh yeah, they'd have big dances with a string band. Dance in the living room and in here, too. They'd take all the tables out," he says, gesturing around the dining room which has become his home, with his bed in one corner, his chair in the middle, and bureaus and sideboards around the walls.

Dances, of course, were not the main business of that room in the past. The Lowes fed the guests bountifully the produce from their farm and gardens.

"We had three hot meals a day. Breakfast would start at six o'clock and go to eight. We'd start out with oatmeal, eggs, bacon, ham, hot biscuits, butter, and jam. Mother was a good cook. You can ask anybody," says Charles.

"Wasn't nothing fancy but it was good eating. We raised our own meat and milk, hogs, sheep, and beef cattle. I worked in the gardens here, raised everything that was eatable: corn, tomatoes, cucumbers, potatoes, everything you ever wanted to eat that grows in this country."

His mother, Blanche, supervised a staff of cooks who prepared meals on large wood cookstoves that were in operation from dawn to dusk.

"They made their own bread and everything. In the summertime the girls from Lees-McRae would all come down and wait the tables," he says, looking around the room that was once so full of guests but is now full of memories.

Outside the hotel the grapevines continue to flourish, climbing the sides of the house to produce rich clusters of purple grapes. Chickens wander about the yard, many generations removed from the large flocks that provided eggs and heaping platters of fried chicken to hungry guests. A few dogs lie peacefully in the autumn sun.

The building is quiet now, closed for good when Charles's sister Fannie died in 1973.

"I've got more kinfolk up there in the cemetery than I've got in Banner Elk now. I just want to keep it like it was. People come every day and want to buy stuff. Why, they'd buy my bed and I would have no place to sleep," says Charles, pointing to his quilt-laden resting place in the corner.

There has been some talk about nominating the building to the National Register of Historic Places, but Charles Lowe simply wants to live out his life in the only home he's ever known. He doesn't want visitors walking all over the place; the shadows of the past are company enough.

Old A. P. Brinkley Store stands abandoned.

ELK PARK

Among the flourishing June weeds from the top of the cemetery knoll, you can look down through the trees to Highway 19-E passing through this small town on the Tennessee border. Where pickup trucks and cars now pass, not that long ago trains chugged along bringing people and goods from Johnson City and taking lumber and ore back.

Many changes have come to Elk Park over the years since the first settlers secured a foothold here near the Elk River. Older residents of the sleepy town have seen it flourish and subside.

"Changes? I've seen seventy-eight years of changes. This was a hub, a shipping place, the biggest place around. But things have changed," says Dick Patton, lifelong resident of Elk Park.

"You're mighty right," says Fred Hughes, nodding his head vigorously.

Patton, Hughes, and Raymond Jones sit in wooden chairs facing the television in Pat Hughes's grocery store. These four men have watched the tide of prosperity rise and ebb in their town over their eight decades of existence.

They've seen the railroad depart and automobile traffic replace it. They've seen industry come and go. They've watched generations of children grow up and leave for more prosperous locations. Patton and the two Hugheses have served as mayor over the years, struggling with fortune's revolutions.

But these Avery Countians have never lost their love of their town and their appreciation for the way of life that continues today along the narrow, quiet streets that branch off from 19-E to ascend the hills and creep into the coves under Hump Mountain.

From their seats in Hughes' Grocery, they monitor the times while they recall their heritage.

"We still can't tell you how old Elk Park is. The oldest marker over on that hill is John Harden—born 1795," says

Dick Patton, Fred Hughes, Pat Hughes, and Raymond Jones stand by Hughes' Grocery, where they sit and watch their changing community.

Patton, pointing across the road toward Tennessee where a small knoll stands above the town.

"He had a slave. Just as you come into town right where this tree farm is—he gave that to his slave, Peter Harden, just at the time of the Civil War. He was colored. It was called the Harden place," he says, and his friends nod their heads.

"Elk Park was incorporated in March 1885. You can see the date on the town hall up here; it's on the front of it," says Patton.

For many years the town was an important stop on the E.T.& W.N.C. Railroad, the Tweetsie. It linked the isolated mountain community to the outer world as well as to the other towns in Avery, Watauga, and Mitchell counties.

"When I was a boy, your bread came from Skelton Bakery in Johnson City. They also loaded ice in a hemp sack; it was packed in sawdust and wood shavings. That was before they built the ice plant here," says Patton.

"See that yellow line?" says Pat Hughes from behind his checkout counter, pointing out the front door to the street. "That's where the train ran."

"I'd like to see it come back," says Raymond Jones, leaning forward to watch an old, green Ford truck rumble along followed by a sleek burgundy Jaguar.

The men watch the town residents go about their business and the summer tourists flow by, most of them going to other places like Linville, Banner Elk, or Boone.

"Used to be there was three big hotels, the Tatum, Walsh, and Avery. They'd be full of people travelling through—salesmen," says Patton.

"They had boarders that boarded, some of them year-round, some shorter, like a school term," says Fred Hughes.

"They'd done a good business," says Patton, shaking his head trying to understand where they'd gone.

"Timber and mines—that was the life of this town. That's why everybody moved into this country. White's was a band-mill on Elk River. Lupert Lumber Company of Pennsylvania was below the Elk Falls. They had a catch pond over Butler, Tennessee," says Patton.

The Cranberry Iron Ore Mines just outside the town also

provided a level of prosperity that faded when the mining ceased.

"The mines closed down on account of cheap ore being brought in here. The timber was cut and gone," says Patton.

"And the Depression times were here. The bank closed. It was a Citizens Bank as I recall," says Pat Hughes, looking over from checking out a customer.

Patton, the Hugheses, and Jones recall other past successes: the Gayola Bottling Plant, the Teaberry Gum Factory, three herb markets that bought and sold ginseng, galax, mayapple, and other forest treasures, an orphanage for black children, doctors, and lawyers—all gone today.

Yet life in the town goes on, pleasantly if not with wild prosperity. William Cable's trout farm provides a few jobs. The shrubbery and Christmas tree industry is flourishing. Area orchards continue to produce world-class fruit. The McClain fence post business thrives.

The Brinkley Hardware Store has been a constant throughout the oldest man's life.

Down the street from Hughes' Grocery, Borian and Blue Blair, Gary Hicks, and Jamie Moody keep the volunteer fire department's equipment shining on this sunny Saturday. They're content with their town.

At the Sunrise Market, Mayor Brenda Cook is enthusiastic about the future.

"We are in the process of building a sewer plant. Hopefully we'll complete it by September 1996. It will process 100,000 gallons a day to serve all of Elk Park and Cranberry, including the new school at Cranberry.

"We hope we'll be able to invite industry, possibly a nursing home. We're interested in anything that will upgrade and get us back where we used to be," says Mayor Cook.

On the edge of town, Claude Quick continues to cut hair; his customers "lose weight the Quick way," as his sign proclaims.

"He ain't afraid to use the clippers. I like him," says Paul Laws as the barber quickly gets his customer's hair in order.

"I do good here. I'm sort of semi-retired now. I work three

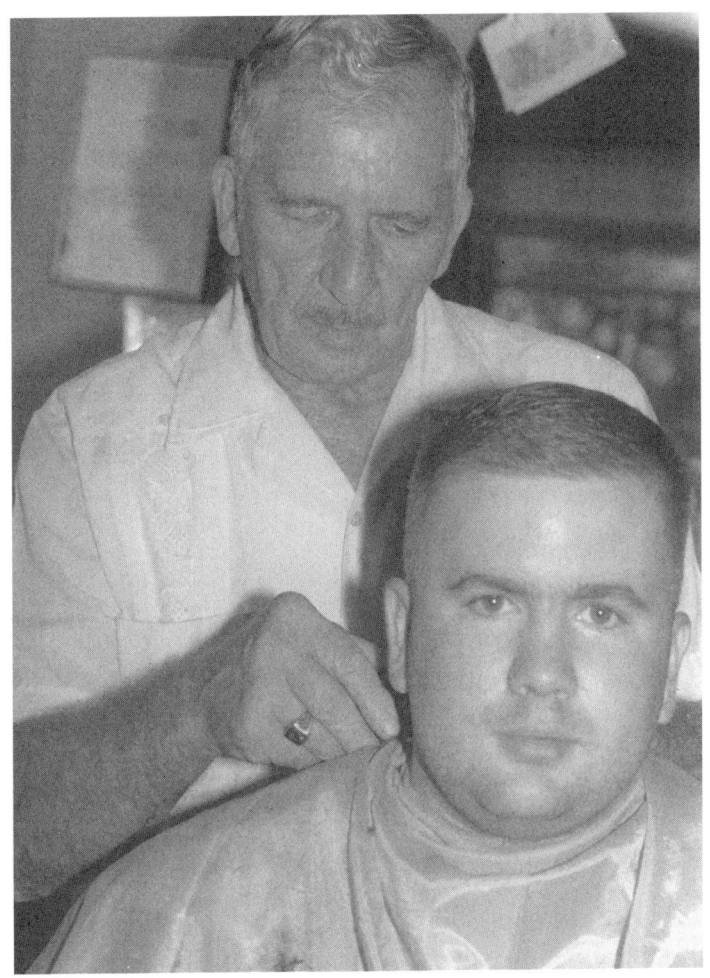

Claude Quick cuts Paul Laws's hair.

days a week, Thursday, Friday, and Saturday, and have plenty of work. I don't care how long it takes to get a haircut, here it's guaranteed to be quick," says Quick as his clippers buzz through Laws' hair.

Mike Smith, Elk Park's policeman for the past eighteen years patrols his town, keeping order and helping his neighbors.

Folks in Elk Park have known prosperity, and they have experienced hard times, but the sense of community and a pride in their heritage have never wavered.

Pam Joslin (left) and Barbara Timberman gather berries in bog.

CRANBERRY BOG

The wealth of the Southern Appalachians has resided for millions of years in the natural resources abundantly showered on the mountains. Today, that wealth has been traded for money—a poor substitute with a limited lifespan—or thoughtlessly destroyed.

Cranberries are an example of the prodigal use of our resources. Known as "rubies of the bog" to early settlers, the cranberry furnished generations of mountain folks with a vitamin-rich food source that with care would last through the winter.

The community of Cranberry, located near the Tennessee-North Carolina border, was named for the tart fruit that grew in a large cranberry bog. Today, the fruit is gone. Mining, logging, and farming gradually destroyed the bog and its riches.

When the iron ore was taken from the mines, the community was left with several large holes in the ground with shafts that run for miles. The one-time bonanza was over at the cost of the destruction of a renewable resource.

Although the *Manual of the Vascular Flora of the Carolinas* shows cranberries in Mitchell County, I have been unable to find anyone who knows where the bog is. Fortunately, in Avery, Burke, and other western North Carolina counties, there are bogs that have survived. The autumn harvest is a tradition that continues today.

Barbara Timberman gathers the ripe berries each fall to provide holiday fare for her family.

"It's best to gather them after the first frost sweetens them. You find a good patch and go to work. You slide your fingers under the bottom of the plant and let the leaves and stems sift through while you snag the berries," she says, as she demonstrates her technique.

Her hands emerge full of the red and yellow berries. They rattle into the bucket as she pours them from her fingers.

"You get a lot of sticks and leaves with them, so you have to clean them when you get home," she says, running her fingers through another clump.

Her friend Dean Taylor has developed a cleaning technique. He waits for a windy day, then lines a wheelbarrow with soft towels before dropping the berries from high above to allow the wind to carry away the chaff.

"He brought me here probably fifteen years ago. He's been coming for a long time. I doubt that he's ever bought a cranberry in his life," she says.

Taylor has always known where to find cranberries. His family has been coming to the same bogs for generations, and he gladly continues the tradition.

"My grandparents and a lot of other people would gather cranberries every year. My grandparents would go to Pineola with wagons and bring back tubs full of the berries," says Taylor, a retired French teacher and lifelong resident of Avery County.

The cranberries grew in such profusion that the harvest

Cranberries fill a bucket with fruit to preserve for winter.

contributed substantially to the family larder during the cold winter months, when folks depended on what they had preserved during the summer and fall.

"To the best of my knowledge, they were kept for home use rather than sale. They'd keep them in a cool, dry place, and they would last for a few months," says Taylor.

For thirty years he has followed the tradition, visiting the remaining cranberry bogs in the county to bring home brimming buckets of berries. Utilizing knowledge handed down from his grandparents, he cooks them up.

"Sometimes they would cook them whole. If you add sugar first, then cook them, they tend to remain whole. If you cook them first then add sugar, they make a sauce.

"Add very little sugar. They have enough pectin to congeal quite well by themselves. The wild berries taste better than the tame ones," he says.

Over the years, the Taylor family has harvested from bogs which continue to produce the autumn bounty. Dean Taylor has also seen some bogs disappear.

"There's one in Pineola, east of the Linville River Bridge, but I think a concrete company dumped old concrete down there and ruined it. Here in Miller's Gap near the high school is a small bog. Formerly there was one near the Cranberry Iron Mines," he says, sighing as he remembers the richness that has been destroyed.

Taylor also knows of cranberry bogs near Mountain City, Tennessee. A recent issue of *The Tennessee Conservationist* features a story on a bog in Shady Valley. The article describes the mountain bogs of the Southern Appalachians as being the cradle of the cranberry.

Many northern plant species, such as the cranberry, were carried south by glaciers during the last ice age. As the ice sheet retreated, it left isolated communities in the high mountains that maintain the cool climate of the more northern states.

From these mountain bogs the cranberry traveled back to the north, where in Massachusetts and Maine it has become an important cash crop.

While some of the cranberry bogs are protected by such groups as the Nature Conservancy, or by being located in a National Forest, others are in danger of casually being destroyed by development.

Nature's gifts which have endured for thousands of years are too precious to be squandered.

Front of Eseeola Lodge seen through timbers of porte cochere.

ESEEOLA

A bountiful nature has given the resort town of Linville beauty and peace which continue to draw families generation after generation. Large hardwood and evergreen trees overshadow thick clumps of rhododendron and laurel, as the murmuring waters of river and stream accompany the whisper of cool breezes through the trees.

One hundred years ago the scene was quite different. While the surrounding mountains were covered with virgin forests and thick vegetation that fascinated visitors, recent logging had denuded the valley.

Avery County writer Shepherd M. Dugger wrote, "In 1891 the ground now occupied by Linville had been cleared and stumped so clean that it looked like a desert bordered with trees. Eseeola Inn sprang up on this like a mirage."

While time and the natural fertility of the mountains have restored the area's rich vegetation, Eseeola has continued to dominate the village, both physically with its imposing construction, and figuratively by being the center of community life.

Eseeola, an Indian word meaning "cliffy river," began as a large, two-hundred-room structure that hosted such nineteenth century luminaries as eminent psychologist William James and novelist and journalist Charles Dudley Warner. It brought to the valley "the finest gathering of high-class people that has ever greeted the opening season of a new mountain place in North Carolina," wrote Dugger.

In 1892, the first of Eseeola's annual Fourth of July celebrations took place. This one included a sack race, a soaped-hog-catching contest, and an ox race. These events allowed local farmers and boys to show their skill and daring as they entertained the less active outlanders.

Getting to the fledgling resort was a physical challenge for the early summer people. Most roads were poor, and the railroad stopped miles away in Cranberry. Families throughout the Southeast found travel to Linville an adventure, at best.

Developers of the resort constructed the Yohnalossee Road, which took its name, "passing bear," from the number of bear traps that the construction crew found along its path. Running from Blowing Rock to Linville, the roadway was a little over a dozen feet wide and eighteen miles long. Local men who worked on the road took great pride in their accomplishment.

"Yes, sir, it was some job. Hewing and grubbing from daylight 'til dark six days a week. Oh, but it was a marvel to behold. There'd never been anything like it in these parts. It was the first road that could be called by that name. And when we got it finished, folks just couldn't believe it," said Joe Hartley, a Linville native who maintained his connection with the resort throughout his life.

Sometime in the mid-1890s Eseeola Inn added a golf course to its attractions, and by 1900 the narrow gauge

Hotel guests Nancy and Jack Doyle play checkers in game room.

Tweetsie railroad penetrated to the resort. Summer cottages began to appear. The community that exists today had begun.

Since those early years many changes have occurred. In 1924, Donald Ross, a famous golf-course architect who had made his reputation at the golf mecca of Pinehurst, laid out a new course for Linville. Over the years the reputation of his course has grown until today it is considered one of the finest in the Southeast.

The Eseeola Inn burned to the ground on July 28, 1936. The wood used in the construction of the inn had dried over the years, which contributed to the rapid combustion of the building. Fortunately, an addition to the inn, the Chestnut Lodge, had been built in 1926. This became the Eseeola Lodge that continues today to be the center of the resort community.

The distinctive look of the lodge comes from the native

trees used in its construction. Chestnut bark shingles cover the sides of the two-story building, and stout logs, complete with bark, frame the porches and the distinctive porte cochere at the main entrance.

Eseeola Lodge takes its design from ideas brought to Linville by Henry Bacon, an architect whose plan for the Lincoln Memorial in Washington, D.C., won him the Gold Medal of the American Institute of Architects. Scattered throughout the area are homes and other buildings either designed by Bacon or influenced by his vision.

Today, the chestnut bark shingles are nearing the end of their functional lives, and the blight that has destroyed the legendary

Ruffin Phillips sits in a chair by the fire in the foyer of the lodge.

mountain chestnut trees makes replacing them a concern.

"It will all have to come off. We are dreading that day. You try to find old chestnut, but there is just not that much around anymore," says John Blackburn, manager of the hotel and president of Linville Resorts.

While locust bark and poplar bark are possible options, the loss of the distinctive chestnut siding that has clothed the building since 1926—and other area homes for even longer—means a loss of tradition that troubles the families who have made Eseeola and Linville a part of their lives for several generations.

But Linville traditions run deeper than the bark.

Unlike most resorts, Linville Resorts Incorporated, with its Eseeola Lodge, is not run to generate profits and provide dividends for investors, but to maintain a way of life handed down from parents to children for years.

"The corporation is primarily people with houses here. We don't pay any dividends; everything we make goes back into the resort to maintain a lifestyle and a peaceful existence. It's been that way since 1944.

"The families have passed it down for generations, and hopefully it will continue that way," says Blackburn, an Avery County native who as a youth worked at the front desk of Eseeola Lodge and returned in 1983 to manage the resort. In 1989 he was named president of Linville Resorts.

Stability is a trademark of today's Eseeola Lodge. For several years it has garnered a Mobil Four Star Resort rating. People return year after year for the excellent cuisine, the famous golf course, tennis courts, and the peaceful ambience of the lodge and the village.

"One lady from Johnson City came for sixty-five years straight—Mrs. Gump. We haven't heard from her for a year or two, and I'm worried," says Blackburn, who knows his guests and the summer residents as friends.

Even the staff feel they are part of the tradition. Juanita Graves at seventy-four years of age has worked for twenty-eight years as a maid at the lodge and cottages. She knows the families and eagerly anticipates the arrival of each new summer season.

"I've got people coming here that been coming a long time. I look real forward to May when we open. I wish I could work the rest of my life here," she says, as she pauses from her dusting in the foyer. She works with careful quietness.

There is a hushed tone to much of the Eseeola's activities. Instead of a band at dinner, the Wilsons play on the grand piano in the dining room. Instead of a floor show, the game room provides checkers and other board games for couples to enjoy before meals. Instead of flashing neon lights, gardens provide bright colors and sweet scents for guests who wander among.

A croquet court, many hiking trails, and a peaceful lake for boating and fishing add to the calm entertainment options at the resort. Nature is the prime entertainer, as she has been for over a hundred years.

For information, write Eseeola Lodge, Box 99, Linville, NC 28646, or call 704-733-4311.

Judge Bill Leavell stands in front of the Mitchell County Court-house that was built in 1907.

BAKERSVILLE COURTHOUSE GHOST

The large white courthouse rises with classical dignity over the Mitchell County seat of Bakersville. Built in 1907, the aging building has held and heard many heartrending stories and bloodcurdling tales. It does not rest quietly at night.

For several years an uneasy spirit has made its presence felt by many of those working in the courthouse. It speaks to courthouse workers, it opens doors, it descends stairs, and it walks restlessly.

"I assume it has some kind of unfinished business," says Bill Leavell, a district judge who has an office in the second story of the building.

In less than a year in office, Leavell has had a couple of experiences that have piqued his interest in the "ghost." The first happened as he worked alone on a quiet afternoon.

"I was up here one Sunday afternoon, and I heard a door slam. I went to see if someone was here. I looked through the whole building, and no one was here.

"I thought it might have been a draft, but all the windows were closed. I couldn't figure out why that door had slammed," says Leavell, as he sits in his office overlooking Highway 226 at the end of the building.

His second ghostly happening came in a crowded courtroom during a trial.

"I was reading the jury instructions. I was about halfway through when I heard someone say, 'Objection!' It's really not proper to object during jury instruction, so I looked out to see who had said it. Nobody had said it.

"It was just really odd. I didn't recognize the voice, just out of nowhere. I couldn't tell whether it was a man's voice or a woman's voice. That's just how Butch describes it," says Leavell, shaking his head as he stands in the courtroom where the voice spoke to him.

Butch is Butch Woody, longtime Clerk of Court for Mitchell County. Since the early 1970s she has worked in the courthouse. At one point that she can't place in time, she began

Judge Bill Leavell

to hear the voice.

"Now I don't remember when I first started hearing it. All it says is, 'Butch,' and I can't distinguish if it's a male or female voice. At first I thought the other girls were calling me, and I'd say 'What?' and look around," says Butch Woody, as she finishes filing judgments after a long day in court.

"I hadn't heard it for quite a while, but I heard it this morning in the courtroom. It happens when—like in the courtroom—there was a lot of people around. I heard, 'Butch,'" she says and swinging her head around as if to answer. "I thought someone wanted me, but no one's there."

She has heard it call her name at night when she is alone,

Mitchell County Clerk of Court Butch Woody.

as well as during the day when people are around. She has also heard it walking around the building when no one was there.

"I don't know if I do or I don't believe in ghosts, but someone is calling my name, and I don't hear it anywhere but in this courthouse," says Woody, calmly but firmly.

When Vernon Bishop became sheriff, Butch told him about her experiences. He laughed at her at first, until he, too, heard the sounds of the restless spirit.

"I'm not going to come right out and say it's a ghost. I'm just saying there's a lot of noise I can't explain," says the sheriff, rocking back in his chair, slightly uncomfortable in talking about a disturbing presence that can't be handcuffed or incarcerated.

"I was in here at ten o'clock one night. I heard someone walk down the back steps in the building. I went out to see who it was, and there was no one there. There wasn't anybody in this building but me. And that's the truth," says Bishop, his unblinking blue eyes looking straight into those of his interviewer.

The sheriff works alone many nights till one or two in the morning in his first-floor office at the courthouse. Some nights the amount of noise becomes almost amusing.

"People walking, doors shutting, chairs squeaking, drawers closing. I used to years ago get my flashlight and look around. I don't even do that anymore—nothing there. I don't pay any attention to it," he says, then chuckles.

In the office next door is Windle Young, the magistrate for twenty-one years. He, too, has had his nighttime work disturbed.

"Back when I worked at night I'd hear a door slam, and then I'd wait for somebody to come in. At three or four in the morning, it'd slam. I'd hear steps and wait for it to continue, but nothing," says the magistrate, shrugging his shoulders.

The only one to have glimpsed the spirit is Kay Woody, the deputy clerk of court. She says she doesn't believe in ghosts, but she admits that some things happen that can't be explained.

"As I was walking down the hall, in the second office I saw a man standing there at one of the file cabinets. I went by, then thought, 'Who was that?' I backed up, and he was gone. I circled through all the offices and there was nothing, no one," she says, slightly ducking her head and opening out her hands.

What she saw wore a white shirt and gray pants, and stood with his back to her. She has also heard his activities.

"I've been sitting at my desk and heard the swinging doors upstairs in the courtroom. I've heard it swing open and hit, then hear it doing this (she demonstrates with her hands how the two doors brush back and forth) then slow down and stop," she says, then explains that she will go upstairs, look around, but see no one.

She has also heard someone start down the narrow set of stairs leading to the second story. There is a switchback in the middle of the stairs. She waits to see who it is.

"No one comes out," she says, shaking her blonde hair and opening her eyes wide.

Several people associated with the courthouse have died untimely deaths in the past quarter of a century, and in the ninety years since its construction there have been many potential haunters passing through its doors.

No one knows who or what the spirit is, but some agree that it is not frightening.

"It doesn't make me fearful at all. It's kind of comforting," says a smiling Butch Woody.

Bill Leavell echoes her words.

"This is not a scary ghost. I don't feel scared being here alone. Actually, it's kind of comforting knowing someone else is here," he says, looking around the well-worn courtroom.

Department of Transportation moved road signs that obscured the museum.

BAKERSVILLE MUSEUM

The small, white, wood frame building has stood in Bakersville as long as anyone can remember, and as far back as photographs record. Standing near the courthouse at the intersection of Highways 226 and 261, it has served the town in a variety of functions.

Appropriately, the building is in the process of becoming the Mitchell County Historical Society Museum. As county residents donate various items of historical and cultural interest, the one-room building gradually fills. The small structure itself remains the most evocative of the artifacts.

"It is one of the oldest buildings in town. We felt like it should be preserved," says Mary Lee Barron, who grew up next door to the building once owned by her family.

Old photographs that she has gathered show the McBee

building, as it became known to the past few generations, standing resolutely on its roadside lot.

One of the oldest pictures shows Cane Creek meandering below the town, occupying a quite different bed than the one it flows through today. Perhaps taken during the 1901 flood, it reveals a wood frame courthouse standing where the present courthouse, built in 1907, overlooks the town.

The only building in the picture that still stands is the humble one that has become the museum. Viewed from above town on the Roan Mountain side, it faced the dirt road and had wooden shingles and a chimney. In those days it had a second story, or at least a window providing ventilation for the attic.

Two other old pictures show the same building from the front. In these it looks more like a store than an office.

"At one time it was a pharmacy, then a store," says Barron, whose research reveals a succession of owners, including her grandparents and her father before John C. McBee bought it to use as his law office.

Mules and buggy stand in front of the museum when it was a store.

A large moonshine still is one of the museum's exhibits.

"McBee, Senior, was a lawyer, and so was McBee, Junior. We got the building through the McBees' granddaughter. Martha McBee Summerour gave it to the Historical Society in the last year," says Barron, who has been involved in extensive renovation of the old building.

Generations of legal papers, too many filing cabinets to count, and miscellaneous junk first had to be cleared out. Then old floor tile was removed, the building rewired, and new windows installed.

"We just put the new door in. Bob Mickles did the gardens and other landscaping, and Red Greene built the window boxes for flowers," says Barron, swinging open the heavy new door.

Inside are traditional symbols of mountain life: a large moonshine still and two spinning wheels, one large, one small. Old pictures, ledgers, newspapers, and other relics which reveal the history of Mitchell County hang on the walls and lie on a large table.

There is an interesting story about the old still, but Barron won't reveal it to the press. All she'll tell is where it came from.

"We inherited it from Rex Wilson, and Rex Wilson inherited it from the Baileys. When Rex got ready to move, he called us and asked us if we'd like to have it for the Historical Society," she says, her eyes twinkling behind her glasses.

The small spinning wheel is on loan from Mary Morgan, while the large one belongs to Barron, who says that having exhibits on loan is one way the society plans to build the museum's inventory.

Mary Emma McBee's Singer peddle sewing machine is on display, as well as the McBees' old safe that was found in the office.

"If anyone has something that you would like to donate, we are looking for more exhibits. It's a Mitchell County thing, so we'll take anything that bears on county history," Barron says.

The museum opened this past summer for the Rhododendron Festival, but it is far from finished.

"We're just in the beginning stages. The next step is painting the outside and getting our display cases up. We have applied for several grants and gotten a few," says Barron.

The state Department of Transportation has moved road signs that obscured the building, and once again it is ready to become an important part of the county's life.

To visit the museum, come to Bakersville on Monday or Wednesday from 10 a.m. to 2 p.m., when Irene Sparks works at the Historical Society office across the street. For information call her at 704-688-4469.

Rambling cabin sits atop ridge above Wing Road. One-room cabin with chimney was the original building.

CABIN IN THE LAURELS

Perched on a ridge overlooking Wing Road between Bakersville and Spruce Pine sits a rambling old cabin. In addition to its rustic beauty and historic value as a cultural artifact, this venerable building once was the home of Muriel Earley Sheppard, author of *Cabins in the Laurel.*

Her book was one of the first accounts of life in the Toe River Valley to achieve wide circulation. Originally published in 1935, *Cabins in the Laurel* was reissued in 1991 with a foreword by area novelist, John Ehle.

Muriel Sheppard's work offended many of her mountain neighbors when it first came out, but over the years it has become accepted, if not welcomed. Coming into the mountains in 1927 with her mining engineer husband, she wrote parts of the book in this weathered cabin that looks across the valley to the Black Mountains.

"I guess this is Mitchell County's best-kept secret," says Sue Askew Stewart, as she lifts the latch to open the door on a cold March morning.

"I inherited it in 1981, and my mother had told me that Muriel Sheppard had rented it back in the late '20s or early '30s. The information had been passed down through the generations," she says, as she leads the way into a medium-sized room paneled with thick planks of knotty pine.

"This is the original one-room cabin. I have a deed that goes back to 1890. That's the original fireplace," says Stewart, pointing to a fieldstone fireplace in the center of the wall

The original chimney stands beside the cabin.

to the left of the front door.

While the precise origin of the original cabin is unclear, it has its story.

"Charles and Josephine White moved into the big white house just down from here. Mr. White brought an upstairs maid—they were having an affair. So Josephine White moved out into this one-room cabin. She got a divorce and a judgment giving her this part of the property.

Black Mountain range stretches across horizon seen from the upstairs bedroom.

"She ended up dying here. She froze to death in front of the fireplace. When she was found, her cat had eaten her nose," says Stewart, shivering in the cold room.

The log house has grown along the ridge over the years, branching out from this first room. To the right of the entrance is a two-story addition with a bathroom and three bedrooms. A narrow staircase climbs to the second story.

The door to the staircase, as well as other doors in the house, is hinged and latched with heavy wrought iron.

"All the wrought iron in the house was done by Daniel Boone IV," says Stewart, referring to a Boone descendant who operated a well-known blacksmith shop in the valley in the middle of this century.

From a window in the small upstairs bedroom, the majestic range of the Black Mountains, home of Mount Mitchell, can be seen on the horizon. Large laurel bushes surround the trees that stretch to the sky, framing the famous range.

Seen from above, the new shingle roof contrasts strongly with the weathered slabs that cover the old cabin's walls. Descending the stairs, Stewart raises the heavy latch to walk onto the porch, where she points to the crumbling mortar chinking.

"This is the original mortar. I've contacted Appalachian State and UNC-Asheville to try to get it tested to determine the age, but they didn't have anyone who did that," she says, running her hand over the aged material.

She then turns and points to an exposed log.

"You can see the original hand-hewed logs in places under the slabs," she says, showing the dovetailed joint where the wormy chestnut logs are joined.

The sturdy original stone chimney still stands at the side of the cabin. The cream-colored coating is chipping from it, but the rocks are still firmly joined.

From that side of the building a long den leading into a kitchen that has been added. Wormy chestnut boards panel the den, which has its own fireplace. Nearby stands a modern house where Sue Stewart and her husband Carl live.

"My mother, Mari Askew Brydon, bought this property in 1968, and we moved down here. After I inherited it, I rented the old house out by the year, but recently we decided to capitalize on its background and charm and rent it by the night and week," she says, leaning against a stone wall which faces the cabin.

Since opening in November 1995, the cabin was rented through January by a variety of tourists. In December the cabin housed visitors from Sydney, Australia; St. Augustine, Florida; and Charlotte, North Carolina.

For information call 800-500-0684 or 828-688-4083.

Steve Wilson looks over his empty pastures and retired milk equipment.

WILSON'S DAIRY FARM CLOSES

Steve Wilson's farm is quiet these days. The last dairy in Mitchell County has closed its milk parlor and sold its cows. The dairyman has found a good job at Unimin, and the cows have found a good home on the Nolichucky River. Even the milk truck has found a new place in Chapel Hill.

But Mitchell County is poorer for the loss.

The decision to close was not an easy one for Steve Wilson to make. A rusting sign at the road identifies the dairy as "Ed Wilson and Son." The farm had been his father's until Steve took it over in 1981. For almost fifteen years he spent all his energy, his intelligence, and his resources on the farm, operating it day in, day out.

In the end, all he had wasn't quite enough. He became the third dairy farmer in a year to call it quits in the Toe River Valley.

"There's two legitimate ways of looking at it. One—those who can produce most efficiently should produce and thrive. On the other hand, there was once twenty-five dairies in Mitchell County, seventy-five in the Toe River Valley. Now there's one left in the whole valley, Berl Austin's over on Prices Creek.

"There was a real way of life. These mountain farms were doing something really worthwhile—good for something, good for the people," says Wilson, leaning against a weathered fence as he looks out over the milking parlor to the empty pastures beyond.

He feels the loss for the community, as well as for his family. What is gone is difficult to articulate, especially in a world where profit margins and growth are the measures of success. Yet, his experience tells him there is more.

"It goes back to the benefits of diversity. Getting down to something as simple as plants—with different grasses and clovers in the pasture, the cows do better. Maybe our society would be better with diversity," says Wilson, his calm voice hiding the intensity of his feelings.

Ed Wilson and his son Steve

Rusting old sign speaks of days past.

Located not far from Bakersville on White Oak Creek, the dairy has been part of the town for generations. Not only did a large part of the $10,000-a-month milk sales end up in the hands of the merchants and bankers at the county seat, there was more.

"The intangibles are what we are losing. If progress is having to work less, maybe we've made progress in this area. But I think Bakersville will be less without the dairy farm up here," he says, running his hand through his thinning brown hair.

After his first week's work at Unimin, a mining operation outside Spruce Pine, Wilson is relieved to have a job that requires only eight hours a day, five days a week. Yet, the past is too much a part of him and his family to simply dismiss the work of a lifetime.

"I can't feel guilty about it because I gave 110 percent seven days a week for years. As far as family tradition, in a way it had become irrelevant. Other factors were weighing on me so heavily I couldn't consider that," he says, as he begins once more to run through the factors that ultimately led to his decision.

Milk prices and price supports were problems that had nagged him for years. High price supports in the 1970s caused dairies to expand, producing a chronic milk surplus.

"Under Reagan the supports were ratcheted down so they were virtually nonexistent. Surplus kept demand from overtaking supply, kept too much milk on the market. Low prices ultimately drove me out; the income was too low," he says.

"Every day I had to do what would make or save me the most money that day. Cows always got fed. Cows always got milked. The milk truck always made the trip to Asheville.

"But fences were not built. Buildings not maintained. Same thing with expensive farm equipment. I just barely kept it running to do what we had to do," says Wilson.

Then this past year feed went up over fifty percent. Bull calf prices dropped from over $100 a head to under $25. Two of the dairies whose milk he was hauling together with his own closed down.

"I felt like I had to be perfect. If I stayed in I had to be a perfect manager; there was no margin for error. Nobody can be perfect all the time. With four kids I couldn't afford to gamble anymore," he says, looking up to the farmhouse that sits on a rise overlooking his pastures, the feed bins which allowed him to purchase larger quantities of feed at a lower unit price, and the milk parlor.

In addition, there were environmental problems. Wilson has always been a supporter of water quality in the county. From no-till planting in his cornfields to controlling nonpoint pollution from his cattle, he was a model farmer.

Over the years the county agricultural agents and the soil conservation specialists would bring journalists and students to Wilson's farm to demonstrate the agricultural practices designed to protect the environment. The 1995 Conservation Field Day was held at his farm, where his conscrvation methods and dairy techniques were lauded.

But he could not continue to practice such effective techniques as spreading manure on the fields for fertilizer.

"Phosphate was building up on the farm. The soil can get phosphate toxic. It starts leaching into the groundwater. Eventually, waste removal would have become a problem.

"If I had more time, equipment, and money, I could have developed a composting system to make potting soil. There were options, but they take money," says Wilson, shrugging his shoulders.

The accumulation of problems pushed the dairyman closer and closer to the edge. Then last winter, the hardest of the century, knocked him over.

"The hard winter really made me wonder if I had to do this for a living. A farm is a dangerous place. A farm under stress is more likely to have accidents. I had to consider my family," he says.

Fortunately, he had an education to fall back on.

"My mother saw to it that I got a four-year college degree. I didn't have to stay in the game until the last card was played. I didn't have to sell the timber or the land.

"I think God's hand has guided this whole transition. The cows went to a happy home. The milk truck is sold to a dairy in Chapel Hill. I had hay to make to carry me through the summer until my job at Unimin started last week," says Wilson, a smile lighting up his face.

The story ends happily for those directly involved. Yet the community has suffered a loss that is incalculable. And the sound of cows lowing to be milked will no longer be heard on White Oak Creek.

A brick base and chiselled stone mark the grave of patriarch Charles McKinney.

CHARLES MCKINNEY: PATRIARCH

While collectors search for antiques or old looms or worn pieces of farm equipment to have a piece of mountain heritage, the blood flowing through the veins of those born in the high valleys of the Southern Appalachians is a living link to the past that endures.

McKinney blood is one of the strongest strains leading back to the early settlement of the Toe River Valley. A glance through area phone books shows the large number of this family's descendants who continue to thrive here. The family patriarch Charles McKinney has left a living legacy.

He was a legendary character. Having at least four wives at the same time and forty-eight children, Charles McKinney created a domain on the Blue Ridge where he has given his name to McKinney Gap, the entry to the Toe River Valley.

A small cemetery a couple hundred yards from the Blue Ridge Parkway near the gap holds several members of the McKinney clan, including the patriarch Charles and one or more of his wives. Tall rhododendron bushes shade the scattered stones that have stood as memorials for over a century and a half.

In recent years members of the McKinney family have placed a brick base and a chiselled stone above Charles's remains, so his tomb looms large overlooking his family's scratched fieldstones. At his death, a neighbor on Three Mile Creek wrote his epitaph.

Uncle Jake Carpenter's *Anthology of Death* contains his commentaries on many individuals, but no other entry is as interesting as that on Charles McKinney. What Uncle Jake's spelling and punctuation lack, his wit makes up for:

A railroad tunnel goes under McKinney's grave.

Charley Kiney ag 72 dide may 10 1852
wars farmer live in mt on bluey rige at kiney gape hey
had 4 wim [women] cors marid to won res live on
farme all wen to felde work to mak gran all wen to
crib   for the brd all wen Smk hos for thare mete
hey cild bote 75 to 80 hages [hogs] eve yere & winon
[women] nuver had worde bot him haven so many
winin he wod be this times wod be hare [hair] polde
(pulled) thar ware 42 childern blong to him th all
went to preching togethern noth set [nothing said]
the des aver bod go long smoth hel won nother [help
one another] hey made brandy all of his lif never had
any foes got long smoth with avery bodi I nod him

According to Estelena McKinney Harper, each of the wives
had her own home where she lived with the children born to
her and Charles. With at least four wives, maybe seven, he
spent a night with each, turn and turn about, in a regular
rotation. In the mornings he rode from house to house to
check on his wives and his numerous progeny.

As Uncle Jake reports, they all shared the field work, and
they all went to a common corncrib for grain and smoke-
house for meat. They got along well, going to church together
and helping one another.

On Christmas the clan gathered at one house for a day of
togetherness. The large group feasted, sang, and spent the
day much as other families, but with a greater scope for their
activities with such a crowd.

"My great-great grandfather must have had a magnetic
personality and the makings of a general to have so many
women to agree to his unusual arrangement and being
happy with it," wrote Estelena McKinney in her book, *Charles
McKinney and Related Families*, in a masterpiece of under-
statement.

Although there are various stories about McKinney's background, tradition holds that he arrived at the Gap with a
wagon load of apple seedlings and a grant for 100 acres of
land. Eventually his holding included 1,200 acres with extensive orchards, cropland, and pastures.

A relative is buried nearby with a formal tombstone.

Today the family graveyard stands high on a ridge that overlooks the old apple trees of the Orchard at Altapass, and in the woods stand scattered ancient apple trees, another enduring part of the McKinney legacy.

The names of his four wives have come down to us, as well as records of the various branches of this strong family tree. Elizabeth Lowery is a legal wife, for there are records of their marriage bond. The other wives may have had formal unions, but if so their records have been lost.

Margaret "Peggy" Lowery was the sister of Elizabeth. These two women perhaps came to the mountains with McKinney.

Sarah "Sally" Hobson was a midwife. She delivered the babies for all the McKinney wives. Nancy Triplett was the last of the four wives.

Sally Hobson told one of her grandsons that Charles had seven wives within a one-mile radius. When he asked why she lived in such an arrangement, she said,"I have all these children—about twelve—by him, and he is very devoted to them, and he provides us a good living."

One story that has come down to the present is about Charles's taking his thirty-five boys down to Marion to buy hats. After lining them up, oldest to youngest, outside Blanton's store, he went in to talk with the storekeeper. When Blanton heard how many hats McKinney wanted, he asked why he needed so many.

Not believing the story that McKinney needed them all for his boys, Blanton told him that if it was true, he would give them the hats. So the patriarch marched his sons into the store. Blanton was as good as his word and gave them each a hat.

Many of the modern McKinneys take pride in their ancestor, but some feel a resentment for his unusual conjugal arrangements. Estelena Harper mentions in her book that a few of his descendants corrected her when she referred to the four women as wives of McKinney.

She defends them as such because the family traditionally referred to them as wives and "they always functioned as a family," with Charles taking responsibility for his children and care of his wives. Finally, "out of respect for my forebarer [sic] and his women I will call them wives. I am very proud of my heritage and would not exchange it for the most illustrious families of the United States," she writes.

Whatever the judgment of today is, Charles McKinney came into the wilderness and turned it into a thriving home for his family. He left not just land and possessions to his descendants, but a strain of pioneer blood that has stood them and their community well over the years. That is true heritage.

This stone pillar, once the toll gate, marks boundaries of Little Switzerland.

LITTLE SWITZERLAND

Sitting astride the continental divide, this resort community has played an important role in the histories of two counties for the past ninety years. Begun as a summer retreat for middle class Carolinians to escape the sweltering heat of the lowlands, Little Switzerland has become a mountaintop escape for lowlanders from throughout the country, as well as a permanent home for the hardier souls who can adapt to winter's cold.

Heriot Clarkson, a Charlotte attorney who later became a North Carolina Supreme Court Judge, rode a mule to the top of Grassy Mountain in June 1909 in the company of two real estate agents. He was so struck with the beauty of the area and its spectacular view of the surrounding mountains and the Piedmont, that he organized nine other investors and by July had signed a contract for Reid Queen and Floyd Gardner, the two realtors, to buy the land from various mountain families.

Reid Queen's son, Reid Queen, Jr., remembers his father's tales of the purchasing of the land from the original families. To mountain farmers used to a barter economy and subsistence farming, the dollar bills looked mighty big.

"They paid from $9 to $35 an acre, and Daddy said that those that got $35 was jumpin' up and down and hollering 'Hooray!'" says Queen.

Anna Twelvetrees, secretary to one of the nine investors D. A. Tompkins, named the budding resort "Little Switzerland," because she agreed with Clarkson that the area resembled the Jura Range of Switzerland, where he had recently visited.

By September 1909, Clarkson and his nine fellow investors incorporated under the name of Switzerland Company. At an average cost of $11 an acre, they held 1,100 acres, 800 of which were in Mitchell County and 300 in McDowell County.

In early 1910 the Company put one hundred lots of an acre apiece up for sale at a minimum price of $150 per acre. This price rose to $300 an acre in 1913. By 1979 the price was between $5,000

The front porch of Heriot Clarkson's house remains today as it was in the early decades of the century.

Judy and Bill Carson enjoy the view.

and $10,000. This past year a lot with an old cottage was sold for $155,000, with the purchaser planning to raze the old building.

"The original concept of Little Switzerland was that everyone got an acre and they could build a tent or a castle, whichever they wanted," says Bill Carson, a year-round resident who is the present president of the Little Switzerland Community Association.

The early homes were usually humble cottages for families. With no electricity, fireplaces were typical. Spring water was carried by gravity from a 1,000-gallon cement tank to the houses by pipes, and there was a sewer system that discharged directly into a mountain stream.

Transportation to the resort was by railroad, with Clarkson using his influence to have the C.C.& O. railroad move its Mt. Mitchell station to just below Gillespie Gap to connect to a rough road to the resort, where a toll road ran from Big Lynn Gap through the resort.

From just a handful of cottages in the early teens of the century, the colony grew to two dozen in the 1930s to over fifty in the 1950s. Today there around 200 homes in the original 1,100 acres.

While the Switzerland Company continued to run the colony for the first several decades, in 1946 the Little Switzerland Community Association was formed to handle some of the responsibilities. In 1949 the organization was incorporated and, since that time, has played a major role in the development of the colony and the management of its resources, particularly the water system.

By the 1970s the character of the community had changed greatly from its earlier years. According to Louisa Duls in her 1982 book, *The Story of Little Switzerland*, even in the 1950s ". . .a common remark by the early settlers, almost entirely from the Carolinas, was 'Those Florida people—they are taking over our resort!'"

According to Duls, instead of families with children who wanted to explore the wonders of the mountains, the new population was largely made up of retired couples interested in handicrafts and cultural programs.

Today it is not an easy task to define Little Switzerland.

"It's like the blind men and the elephant. You have to get several opinions before you can understand the community," says Bill Carson, referring to the fable of the blind men who each felt parts of an elephant and, from holding the trunk or tail or massive leg, tried to define the beast.

Carson and his wife, Judy, visited Little Switzerland back in the 1960s but became involved with the community about twelve years ago. Since becoming permanent residents four years ago, they have seen the need for community cooperation that recognizes the changes that have come throughout this century.

The original 1,100 acres is now surrounded by a larger community, which Bill Carson calls "Greater Little Switzerland." With 400 to 500 homes, this "greater" community has an important role to play in planning the future.

"The Little Switzerland Community Association is a legal entity set up to provide water for the community. It was and is confined to 1,100 acres. The distinction between the historical Little Switzerland and the Greater Little Switzerland is blurring now, because we are becoming a better integrated community.

"When you read things in the paper now about land use and committees being formed, you're talking about Greater Little Switzerland," he says, looking out from his mountain-top home across a vista that reaches into South Carolina.

Carson refers to the various attempts of the community to organize and develop some land use strategies to provide direction for future development. For decades the residents have depended upon restrictive easements in the property deeds to protect the area from rampant commercialization, but in recent years events have occurred that have cast doubt on the reliability of the covenants.

A particular instance of these problems is the construction of a home in an area considered protected by the Blue Ridge Parkway's scenic easements.

"With the stroke of a pen the Parkway Superintendent can negotiate away easements. This rekindled my interest and the community interest in what we could do to protect ourselves.

"We are trying to reach community consensus about the direction the community is going to head," says Carson.

For decades the original area residents were disenfranchised by the "outsiders" who came in with the development, but today the native mountain folks and the permanent residents and summer people of the resort have the chance to create a coherent vision for the future and to provide ways to enforce that vision.

Little Switzerland remains on the same divide it has always occupied, but now it is heading in a different direction than that envisioned by the Charlotte attorney ninety years ago.

For more information contact the Mitchell County Chamber of Commerce (828-765-9483).

The old English Inn.

ENGLISH INN

Many years have passed since visitors found lodging and board at the English Inn not far from the North Toe River that runs through Spruce Pine, a city built by minerals and the railroad. At one time the Inn was the city; today it stands as proudly as ever but lost on a side street and kept as a private dwelling.

One of the first buildings to be constructed in the Toe River Valley, the English Inn has played an important role in many of the most significant events in the history of the area. According to an article written in 1958 in *National Geographic*, the first part of the structure was built in 1765, and the Overmountain Men rested there on their trek to King's Mountain to fight Ferguson and his men.

At that time the Toe River Valley was frontier, a barely

explored land sheltered by the high mountains that kept it a pocket of wilderness between the settlements of the North Carolina Piedmont and East Tennessee. Yet the Inn gained a foothold on a primitive road not far from Gillespie Gap, which gave entrance through the Blue Ridge to the rich valley beyond.

Over the years the Inn prospered as it became a welcome oasis where the road from Marion to Bakersville and then to the Tennessee border crossed the road from Burnsville to Cranberry. The Bailey family acquired the property sometime in the early nineteenth century, then in 1866 James Bailey sold it to Isaac English, whose name the Inn took and has never relinquished.

English raised his large family of eleven children in the rambling old Inn, expanding it when necessary as it became the area's post office, as well as the center of the community's life. In the thick log walls of the Inn is a small door with

Original fireplace where English family cooked is still the focus of the dining room.

a latch with a box behind it. This is where the mail was dropped in the Inn's heyday.

In addition to running the Inn, Isaac English began the mica industry that continues in the district. The large two-story log structure at the end of the building was constructed by English to house his mica plant where workers processed the mineral.

According to a 1931 article by Muriel E. Sheppard, English was fascinated by the many minerals and gems of the area, keeping a collection in the chinking between the massive square-hewn logs of the Inn. When he discovered mica, then known as isinglass, in the area, he was immediately aware of its commercial value but uncertain how to exploit it. Fortunately, an act of patriotic heroism he had performed during the Civil War unexpectedly rewarded him with the advice and support he needed.

As were many of his neighbors in Western North Carolina, English was a Union sympathizer. At one point during the war, he sheltered, fed, and helped to flee to safety four Union soldiers who had escaped from a Confederate prison camp near Columbia, S.C. Risking his life, English had personally guided the men to a Union force under cover of darkness.

One of these men, Col. J. M. Gere, contacted him after the war, moved to the area, and helped him establish his mica business. With a prosperous Inn and a growing mineral business, the English family became the center of Spruce Pine life.

The most hectic days at the English Inn were also its last days of prosperity. In the early years of the twentieth century, the Inn housed the many workers and speculators involved with the building of the railroad to Spruce Pine. The thirteen bedrooms of the Inn were overfilled, the porch that ran the length of the building crowded, and the dining room strained to accommodate the hungry visitors.

But with the railroad station established some distance away on the opposite bank of the North Toe River, the focus of town shifted from the English Inn. Listed as twenty-six years old in the 1860 census, Isaac English died at sventyseven years of age having left his name to the Inn and the mica industry to the future of his town.

Muriel E. Sheppard's description of the Old English Inn in her book *Cabins in the Laurel*, 1935, describes the building as having fallen into disrepair, with sagging doors and general deterioration. The main road no longer ran by the Inn, and a new bridge took traffic across the river.

However, in 1937, the Deneen family from Johnson City, Tennessee, bought the Inn and spent much time and effort restoring it. Maintaining the building and grounds has become a labor of love.

"Mamaw was upset by *Cabins in the Laurel*, what they wrote about the place," says Bennie Deneen Bryan, speaking of her first husband's mother, Mrs. Walter F. Deneen, who lavished time and attention on the old place.

"She bought it in 1937 and worked on it for a year putting up fences, bringing in dirt, and fixing up the yard. She furnished it with antiques and got it all fixed up," says Bennie Deneen Bryan, sorting through documents and articles about the place she has treasured for years.

Helen Deneen, Walter Deneen's daughter, reopened the English Inn for business in 1939, but since that year it has been preserved as a retreat for the Deneen family. The Walter Deneens spent every summer there.

"They lived there from early April, as soon as the last hard freeze had past, until late in October. They loved it there, and my husband loved the place. He was in the process of buying it from his mother when he died. He said, 'Well now, I want it. I want to keep it in the family,'

"I bought it in the spring of 1964," says Bennie Deneen Bryan, whose family continues to occupy the ten furnished bedrooms during the summer.

There have been several changes over the years, some necessitated by convenience and others by city road work. The old springhouse that stands at the opposite end of the building no longer functions. In the past, cool water circulated from a fountain pipe outside the door of the springhouse, through two wall-length troughs.

A picture of the Old English Inn taken in 1900 shows essentially the same building that stands today.

"Lying in the bedroom listening to that water trickling through was so relaxing. And the virgin woods around you made you think you were away from everything," she says.

But in constructing roads the city cut the virgin timber, filled in the spring, and destroyed the pipes that fed the springhouse. It is now used as a storeroom.

The Deneens added wrought iron hinges, latches, and balconies made by the well-known Burnsville blacksmith, Daniel Boone VI, descendant of the famous pioneer. Mrs. Deneen converted old stagecoach lanterns to electric power to provide illumination at night and added a second-story porch that runs the length of the building.

Yet there are many traces of the old days. In a screened-in room midway down the long main building on the first floor, bits of newspaper, turned black by time, still cling to the hewn logs and chinking, relics of a time when newspapers served as wallpaper.

The large dining room fireplace still provides welcome heat on cool nights, although most of the cooking is done in an added on kitchen, rather than on the hearth as in Isaac English's early days. The Deneen family will pop corn in a basket over the open fire, and occasionally roast some meat in an old, handled grill, but the antique cooking utensils are mainly for show.

Traces of the mica business, an industry that the Deneen family pursued for several years themselves, lie in the ground.

"If you do any digging, like I did when I planted flowers, you find mica everywhere," says Bennie Deneen Bryan, who then holds out an old picture of the Inn from days long gone, before her family owned it.

The building remains essentially the same. Anchored at one end by the square, two-storied, hewn-log mica processing plant, now a living room, the long structure stands firmly in front of a steep hillside. A board fence rather than today's picket fence runs across the yard, and there is a horse tethered to the hitching post by the front gate.

Then as now it was a piece of history and a haven. As Bennie Deneen Bryan says, "It's a sweet old place. It's been there so long."

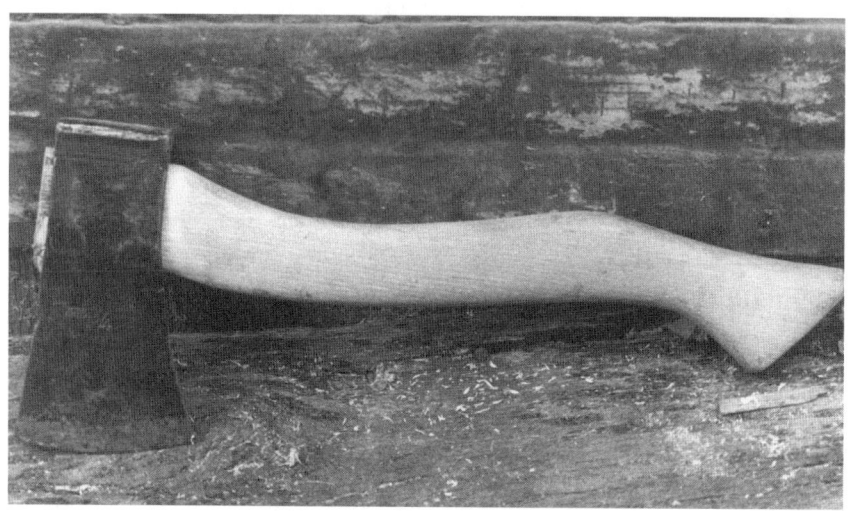

Hand axe with "patented" Willis handle shows his skill.

JOE WILLIS: HANDLEMAN

Joe Willis has carved handles out of hickory for more years than he can remember. He doesn't exactly know when he began, for some of his earliest memories are of carrying in the hickory logs for his father to work on.

If you ask him how long he's been putting sharp steel to hard wood, he says, "That I can't tell you. I helped Dad off and on at it; otherwise I'd help him get the timber. We'd carry it in on our own shoulders.

"He'd tell me to split it, and he'd go to making. I could chop it out with an old axe, but I couldn't hew."

When he started on his own, he turned to a different line of work. As a young man Willis went into lawn care and gardening for the fancy homes springing up around Grassy Creek.

"I worked for the women all the time. They was the ones home telling me what to do. I would whittle on a handle off-and-on, but mostly I mowed yards and kept gardens," he says, dressed in Pointer overalls, a blue work shirt, and black laced boots.

But when his father came to him and asked for help with the handle-making business, Willis couldn't refuse. He joined the old man in making sledgehammer handles for the new mines opening around Spruce Pine.

"When they started the flotation mines over here on the chalk in the late '40s or early '50s, they had a bunch of men with sledgehammers breaking rock. Dad came and said, 'You're going to have to help me make handles.' I got piddling at it until I got pretty good," says Willis, his hazel eyes twinkling behind his glasses.

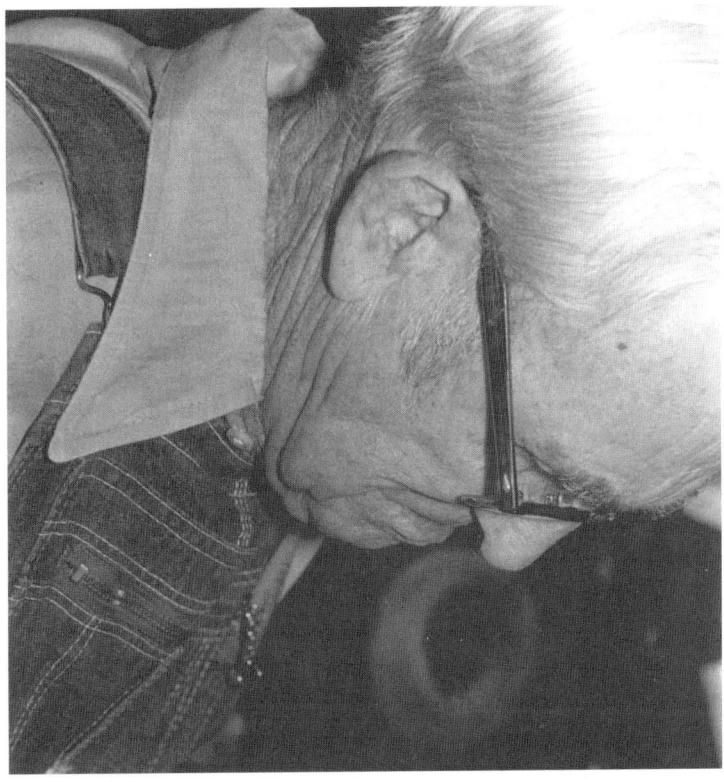

Joe Willis bends to do the fine work with his drawknife.

Under the watchful eye of his father, Willis learned his craft through hard work. He'd show his handles to the master handle-crafter, who would critique them.

"Dad'd tell me what was wrong and how to fix it," he says, running his fingers through his neatly combed silver hair.

In addition to teaching his son the skills of working with hard wood to make handles that will last, the older Willis taught him a philosophy of work that has shaped his life for over a half century.

"Dad always said a half done job ain't no job. If you ain't

Joe Willis uses a double bitted axe to work on a piece of hickory in his woodshed.

going to do it right, the best thing is to go off and rest and don't even try," says Willis, opening the door to the woodshed next to his workshop.

"At the time I thought he was kind of contrary. But I've learned he was right," he says, picking up a double bitted axe and placing a chunk of hickory on the chopping block in the shed.

"People brag on my handles being so smooth and all, and that's where I got it. Now they ain't all perfect, but if I had my way they'd all be perfect.

"The other thing Dad always told me, 'Know where you're going to hit before you strike,'" says Willis, who chops cleanly through the hard wood.

He holds the axe out to show its handle. He bought the axe back in the early '50s, "paid five dollars for it." It wasn't long before the store handle split on him.

"I went into the woods and cut a tree down and carved this handle out of it," he says, showing how the axe blades are nearly worn out, but the handle is as stout as ever.

Then he picks up a heavy go-devil that he splits heavy chunks with. He explains that his dad made the handle for it in 1945. For over fifty years Willis has split wood with it.

"You can't imagine how many logs I busted with that. I've wore out two wedges," he says, running his work-hardened hands up and down the smooth hickory handle.

Stepping outside, Willis walks over to his workshop and unlocks the door. Inside, handles of all kinds surround the big-bellied woodstove and well-worn shaving horse. The carver sinks into his low chair and turns to stuff hickory shavings into the mouth of the stove.

Soon the crinkling iron throws off a warm glow that keeps the chill of autumn outside. The burning wood does a double job; handles on a drying rack are curing above the heating stove.

Covering his legs with a sawdust and wood-shaving covered piece of burlap, he slips a rough stick of hickory under the white oak clencher of his sourwood shaving horse. Clenching the piece of hickory on the shaving horse, he quickly goes to work with a drawknife.

In just a few minutes, Willis turns the piece of kindling into a shapely backscratcher, something he has recently added to his inventory of useful wood products.

"Viven Phillips is the one who started me off on this. She asked me if I could make one," he says, pointing to a drying rack where about forty of the back scratchers are drying into shape with the business ends curved around to a cupped hand shape.

"I said, 'Gal, I can't make back scratchers.' She said, 'Yes you can. Make me fifty.' This was about Thanksgiving. About two weeks before Christmas I got them made. I put them in a bag and took them and dumped them on her desk," says Willis, who now sells more back scratchers than any other single item.

One man who came to get an axe handle left with 200 of the handy scratchers. Willis chops them out with his axe, shapes them with the drawknife, smooths them with a rasp and a broken piece of glass, and carves the teeth with a small knife. He then wets the scratching end and bends it to dry into its finished shape.

Bud Phillips, owner of Mitchell Lumber Company, supplies Willis with the raw material of his trade—large pieces of select hickory. Many of the handles that he makes end up in the lumber yard or in the woods in the hands of Phillips's timber-cutters.

Willis stands to show a peavey that he has fitted with a handle with "Mitchell" written on the white wood. Throughout the shop are handles fitted to metal with initials identifying the owners. Each one is smooth and shapely, fitting the hand well.

"I smooth all the handles with a piece of glass. I take a piece of glass just big enough to hold. When it gets dull, tap it on a piece of metal and break it. That's how you sharpen it," says Willis, demonstrating his finishing technique.

Standing around the shop with new handles are post-hole diggers, pitchforks, shovels, peaveys, mattoxes, axes of all kinds, hammers, crosscut saws, grab-skip hammers, tobacco stick mauls, and a monkey wrench.

"I've made handles for tools that I've never seen before or since, but I've never made a fudge on one of them. You have to use your judgment and ask somebody if you can't figure it out," he says, picking up a strange-looking axe. It has wings that fold out as the blade goes into wood.

"It's supposed to be for splitting wood, but it don't work. I put the handle in anyways, because the man wanted it," he says, shaking his head at the unlikely contraption.

He shows a broadaxe with an offset handle, a hatchet with a handle of his own "patent" curved to strike just right, a pole-axe with a similar unique handle, and a sky-hook, a small piece of wood that holds objects in a way that appears to defy gravity. He then reaches for a small, pointed piece of wood piercing a small leather strap; it's a corn-husker.

He also makes singletrees, spreads and other pieces of workhorse equipment, and walking canes. While he has given up making gunstocks, plow handles, and sneeds for scythes, there is not much a man could want made out of hickory that Willis can't carve. He continues to try his best to do it right.

"They say practice makes perfect. Now I've had a lot of practice, but I'm not perfect," he says, going back to work with a piece of broken glass.

Luther Thomas rests, as his handmade brooms hang beside him.

LUTHER THOMAS

Under gnarled weeping willow trees not far from the small village of Micaville, Luther Thomas wields his Case pocket knife to turn birch saplings, small poplars, and a variety of other forest objects into functional works of art. The skills he uses have been passed down over many generations.

Luther Thomas has spent a lifetime on Cane Branch. During that time he has become as much a part of the natural world of the forest and streams and mountains as the materials he works with. Part of the skills he has inherited is the ability to see the wonders around him and recognize the individual beauty in rocks and burls and fallen trees.

When asked, he can't exactly remember when he began making his mountain crafts, but he knows it was a long time ago.

"It was too long ago. I'm as old as dirt, so as far as I know as to year and date—I don't know. I do remember that I was one of the original eleven who started the little crafts fair here in Burnsville forty years ago," says Thomas, sitting back in his well worn-work chair to rest a moment from his broom making.

Behind him a couple dozen of the finished brooms hang with their business ends neatly cinched with hickory bark. By the window a small chain suspends walnut shells which he has shaped into wee baskets. To his right is a table loaded with finished poplar buckets. And all around the room lie burls, grapevines, and other woodland objects shaped into pieces of art.

The brooms he makes come in a variety of sizes. The smaller ones, about a yard long, are popular as decorations. He leaves the bark on them. They are mostly made from yellow birch, and the smooth, shiny skin catches the light streaming in the windows this unseasonably warm, sunny morning. The longer ones are as tall as a woman, and meant to be used.

"My mother taught me how to make them and how to use them. She made them and showed me how when I was about twelve or thirteen years old. I know what to do with one.

"She'd go to the creek and get creek sand, then get ashes from the fireplace. She'd heat water in

Luther Thomas works on broom handle.

her tub and cut up lye soap in it. Dip it out and keep the floor wet; get the mop wet and scrub around," says Thomas sitting and holding the smooth handle of a long buckeye broom.

"It gets it almost white as snow. If I missed a place that big [he holds his hands a foot apart] she'd see it," he says, then chuckles at the memory.

He explains that the buckeye brooms are handy because they are so light, but that most of them don't turn out. "You might start fifteen to twenty to get two brooms," he says.

Witch hazel also makes a nice broom, but the wood tends to crack when it seasons. The yellow birch makes a good, functional broom that almost always works out beneath the blade.

The long brooms take much more work than the shorter hearth brooms. Once the bushy broom head is made, he must take his knife and skin the handle, rounding it and smoothing it.

"It takes me about as long again as a short one; that's why I make more short ones. A lot of people like the colored bark, too," he says, as he automatically begins to work down the long handle with his yellow-handled Case knife.

He opens his palm to show the knife.

"I wore out a many of them. I want a Case knife. If a knife don't hold a good edge, I don't want it. I just as soon get shet of it," he says, showing the wear on the sharp blade.

Swinging from his clothesline outside is a long broom that shows more than a bit of wear itself. It's his household broom, one that he has used for fourteen years. He believes in the functional aspect of his work. His brooms and buckets can be used and reused.

His skill in making poplar buckets he traces back to his father.

"Me and my daddy used to prospect and mine, and we'd be here in the mountains prospecting of an evening. We'd run into huckleberries or raspberries or blackberries. We'd just step over and skin off the poplar tree to make a bucket to carry them home in," he says, taking up one of the buckets to show its white oak strip around the top and the hickory bark handle and lacing.

"I do this and go to the fairs to let people see what the old people had to do with. You couldn't just go to the store and buy something. You had to make do with what you had to work with. I did.

"I went to housekeeping in an old one-room log house way back on the side of the mountain in 1933," he says, thinking back to the early days of his marriage.

In addition to his participation in the Burnsville Crafts Fair, Thomas has attended the North Carolina State Fair for many years. In 1988 he won the gold medal there for the outstanding craftsman. He also demonstrated his work at the Knoxville World Fair, where he carved hickory flowers and displayed his buckets.

Thomas gets his raw materials by wandering though the National Forest in the area. He has a permit to get the poplar and birch that he uses to make his crafts. He carries his knife and a bowsaw, and he pays attention to his surroundings.

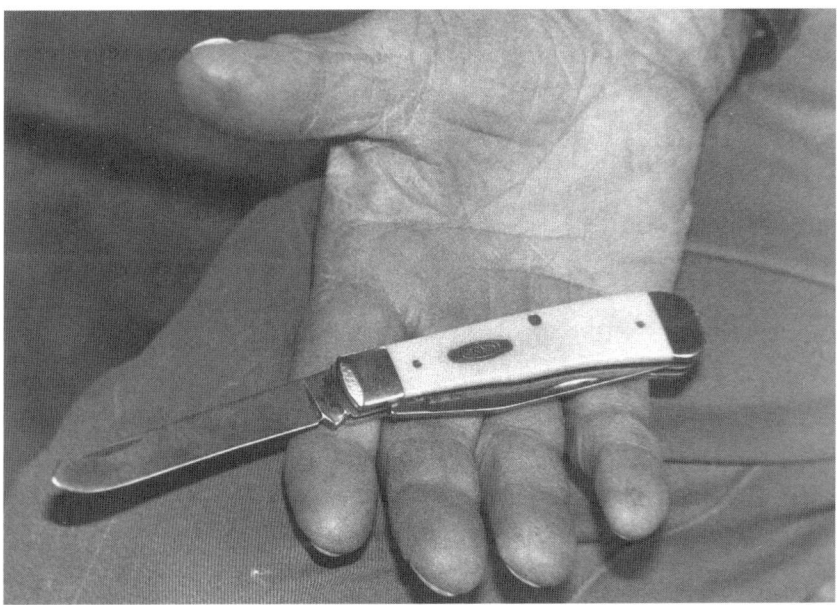

Luther Thomas shows his case knife that he uses for his brooms.

As he searches for the right saplings for his purpose, he notices the rocks and trees surrounding him. He has found some burls that defy belief and some rocks that hold priceless gems.

"I'll be getting brooms or something, and I'll see an oddity and cut it off. Law, law, if I had saved every one I'd found, it'd make a sight," he says, holding up a burl shaped like a turtle.

He displays the oddities that he has found, along with gemstones and minerals and Indian artifacts. He has some unique items that the Smithsonian Institution would like to get their hands on—to go with some of the material they have already obtained from him—but he would rather keep the stones where the local folks can see them.

Luther and his wife, Beatrice, used to sell their crafts and gems and oddities, but since Bea has had to move to a nursing home, Luther has been told by the Social Security people that he can't make an income from his crafts. So he doesn't sell anymore. But he continues to work.

He plans to give his brooms and buckets to his children to do with what they wish. The necessity and salvation of work remains the same for him.

"I'm going to keep working here, keep working. If I give up, that'll be the end," he says, then smiles as he puts knife to wood once again.

L-R: Jerry, Frank, and Faye Griffith, along with Todd Bennett wait on customer.

GRIFFITH'S STORE IN TIPTON HILL

Where can you go to find horse collar pads, post-hole diggers, overalls, bandaids, a can of tuna fish, or a homemade sandwich, lantern wicks, fan belts, wash tubs, rubber boots, feed for cattle and hogs and chickens and sheep and fish and goats and gamebirds and horses and rabbits and dogs and cats, and a whole lot more?

For half this century, Frank Griffith's store has provided the upper end of Mitchell County—and far beyond—with everything needed to survive and thrive in rural society. While the establishment began on a small scale, it grew rapidly, fueled by enterprise and enthusiasm.

"I had a brother-in-law, Farrell Tipton, that was a beginning partner with me in January 1947 over on Brummet's Creek. It was a kind of general store. Also, we more or less did what you call peddling.

"We bought Irish potatoes, give a dollar a bushel, and took them all the way over to Kingsport to peddle them for a dollar-and-a-half. November 19, 1947, we moved to this location," says Frank Griffith, on a warm Saturday evening as customers wander around the goods-packed store.

The original building was torn down in 1955 so the present forty-four feet by one hundred twenty feet store could service area folks. A short way down the road a large warehouse that holds feed, fertilizer, and other bulk items also wears the Frank Griffith name.

Griffith married Faye Ellis on June 18, 1948, and with her support, the business began to grow beyond the grocery and dry goods beginning. Frank and Faye Griffith and Farrell and Blanche Tipton saw the potential and were willing to work to realize it.

"I started working immediately in the store," says Faye, coming up to stand by Frank after making a customer a sandwich.

The old store was torn down in 1955.

"We began to diversify into farm supplies. Our first order of fertilizer, I got to trying to get a fertilizer franchise. The first company turned me down, probably thought I couldn't pay for it—only a little place here.

"The old V-C, Virginia-Carolina, Fertilizer people first sold to us. I always had a warm spot for them and brought from them until they went out of business," says Griffith, standing by the computer that for three years had kept track of customers and accounts.

In 1952 the business received a Purina feed franchise which continues today.

"I guess I'm about the oldest Purina franchise dealer in the Charlotte area, I believe they say. I never thought it at the time," says Frank, shaking his head in wonder at his own success, or longevity.

In addition to hard work, shrewd marketing contributed to their success.

"We used to have free chick day. You got ten chickens with every twenty-five pounds of feed. Nobody would get just 10 chicks, most would want a hundred. We'd get 4,000 to 4,500 chickens the day before," says Faye, her eyes laughing behind her glasses.

"Cars would be parked in the schoolyard and up and down the road. By the end of summer, you know how much feed those full-grown chickens were eating?" says Frank. "They'd buy more feed to feed those chickens."

Feed became a mainstay of the store, and not just because of the free chick day. Cattle feed, horse feed, and hog feed flowed into and out of the large storeroom.

"In those days we sold so much dairy feed; every family had at least one milk cow. There were twenty-two Grade A dairies in Mitchell County, and about everybody made Grade C milk.

"They raised hogs; everybody had some hogs. That was a lot of feed. We had to buy our feed by the railroad car—two railroad cars a month," says Frank.

Fortunately for the storekeepers, the local young men looked forward to the arrival of the railroad cars so they could

Frank, Faye, and Jerry Griffith stand in front of the store.

build their muscles. There were no weight machines or spas in those days, so hefting fifty-pound sacks of feed served the purpose.

Delivering the feed was an important part of their service. The two couples worked hard. "You'd never get any young man to work like that now," says Frank.

"We had a feed run that we made every week to Little Rock Creek, McKinney Cove, Snow Creek, Mine Creek, and Bakersville. I remember taking a seven-ton load up to the head of Greasy Creek—could hardly make it up that road," says Frank.

Delivering groceries was also important. Not everyone had a car in those days, so the storekeepers had to service that need.

"We had several families that came once a month. They'd

buy a full load, and we'd drive it out to them. One family used fifty pounds of meal and fifty pounds of flour each month," says Faye.

"Every week we'd buy 200 twenty-five-pound bags of flour and the same of soup beans," says Frank.

"We certainly have seen a lot of changes. Used to be all gravel roads—no telephone lines. REA [Rural Electrification] hadn't spread into the hollers," says Faye.

But when REA arrived, the Griffiths added another line to their already enormous inventory. They began to sell appliances.

"We even moved refrigerators across the river in boats. I remember one time we loaded two refrigerators and a range on a boat to cross the river at Poplar Station. There was no other way to get it over there," says Frank, appearing amazed now at the things that he did as a matter of course years ago.

The Griffiths and the Tiptons employed only one man to help them. Paul Street worked for them for over thirty years, helping with deliveries and other chores. In 1964 the Tiptons withdrew from the business, leaving the work for their partners. Yet there was always a pool of casual labor to draw from.

"What the secret was—if I needed emergency help, I'd go back to my big stove where all the boys were sitting around. I'd pick some to help us; they were always willing," says Frank.

Today the Griffiths' son, Jerry, runs the business. Although they still work with him, his parents turned it over to him completely about ten years ago. He literally grew up in the store, and as he says, "That's about all I've ever known."

"I guess that I've just tried to follow up on what Dad's done over the years. I guess Dad'd make a good diplomat. I've got a lot of business. I sure do. I'm thankful for it," says Jerry, leaving his assistant Todd Bennett to run the cash register.

"The long hours in the store business is the hardest thing. seventy-two hours a week is a lot in any business. I'm usually here at 6:30 in the morning; then it's 6:30 at night when I get home, until spring, then I'm home later.

"Farmers don't pay much attention to the clock," he says, in between bantering with a customer who wants a free Griffith Feed Store cap and a calendar.

When asked if he knows everything that he has in stock, and where it is, he gives a partially positive answer.

"Yeah, generally I do. I might have to hunt for a while to find it, but I can generally say 'yes' or 'no' if I've got it," he says, his eyes looking around the building, where every inch of space holds some item.

To visit the Griffith Store, turn off Highway 226 in the Red Hill Community of Mitchell County and follow Highway 197 to Tipton Hill. You can't miss it.

Erna sits on her sofa with her daughters.

ERNA HORTON

Erna Horton knows how hard life can be. As she approaches her 101st birthday, her blind eyes give her the first rest from work that she has ever known. But while she can see little in the present, pictures of the past flow clearly through her mind.

Her frame house in the Bailey Settlement of upper Mitchell County—not far from the Tennessee state line—has been her home for many years. She has raised ten children here, and grew up herself not far away. Her home is the community.

"I've been here a long time. I worked hard. I've been on a farm my whole life, never worked a public job," she says, sitting forward on the couch in her living room, her vigorous white hair pulled back from her high forehead.

In 1895, Erna Horton was born right across the hill, "over there," she points, her blue eyes staring sightlessly past her finger "in an old log house." Her great-grandmother Phoebe Bailey was the midwife. From the start her life was hard.

Erna Horton's earliest memories are of work for the family.

"We had work to do. I had something to do at home. Ever since I was big enough to tend to babies, I've had babies to tend for," she says, recalling the younger children she helped to raise in her family and for neighbors.

Farm work also occupied her time. She worked in gardens and took care of the stock from the time she could walk. Feeding chickens, cows and their calves, sheep, turkeys, and

In this photograph taken when she was fourteen years old, Erna Peterson Horton stands on the far right.

horses was a daily ritual.

She started milking cows when she was seven years old. Often she would be a mile or two from her house, out in the fields milking the cows where they stood. She remembers thunder and lightning scaring her as she carried her bucket through the large pastures.

"I had a little wooden bucket made out of cedar. Daddy had bought apple butter in it. One day I was milking out in the pasture, had the bucket almost full.

"My mother came over the top of the hill. The cow saw her and kicked over the bucket. It rolled down into the swamp. I cried and cried," says Erna, recalling the responsibility and the effort, and the frustration.

When her father worked for the railroad, her job was to carry his dinner to him. At nine and ten years old, she stopped to watch as the men labored to drill dynamite holes into large boulders. Her father sharpened the steel tips of the drills that work-hardened men pounded into the rock.

"It all had to do with manpower. They'd take this big old iron and stand it on the rock. They'd be two men on the sides and one holding the iron. One would hit with a big hammer, the man holding would turn it a little, then the other hit it.

"That way they'd drill down into the big, big rocks and put in the dynamite. Then they'd run way off when they shot that thing. Smoke rolled and rocks flew," she says, remembering both the excitement and the fear—and her father's constant hard work.

"You could almost wring the sweat out of his clothes when he came home at night," she says, shaking her head slowly. "He got ten cents an hour, a dollar a day for ten hours."

School had to wait on her work. Even though the school sessions were short, her chores at home took precedence.

"We just had three months of school, when I went to school. And I didn't get to go much. With Daddy working on the railroad, we had to do at home. Mother was just a little woman, wore number three shoes, weighed ninety to ninety-eight, one hundred pounds," she says.

Sunday School filled Erna's day off. Going to church and

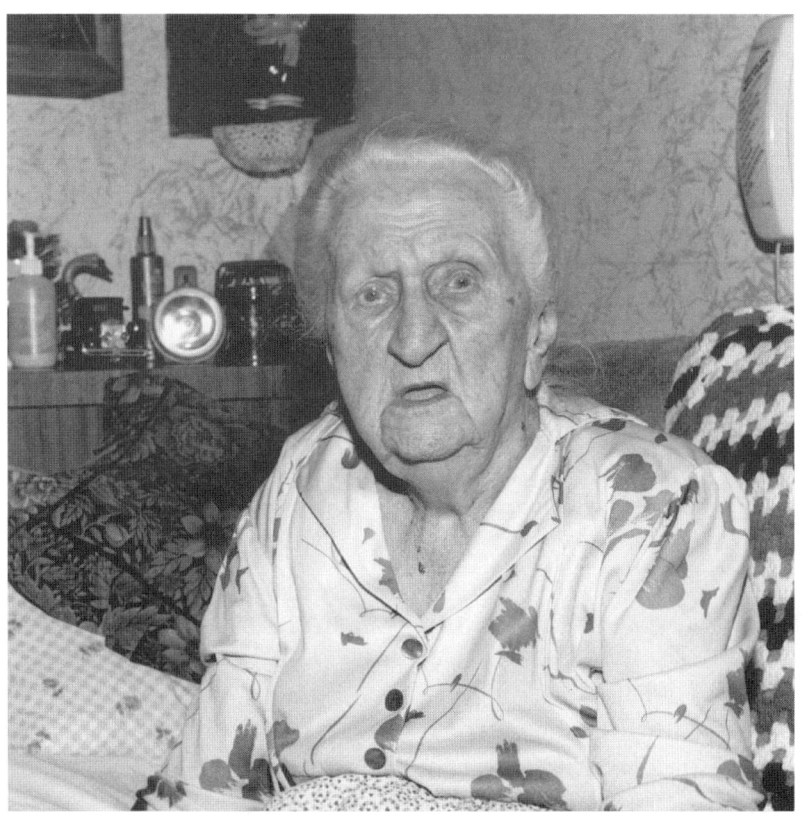

Erna Horton describes the hard life of the mountain woman.

going to the settlement store were the only "traveling" she did. She never went as far as the two closest cities, Burnsville or Erwin, until well after she was married. "I did go to Pigeon Roost," she says, mentioning a small community just around the corner from Poplar.

"Everyone wanted me to help with their babies and children. I was always working for someone. I told Mom, 'If I have to go and wait on everyone, I'll just get married and wait on myself,'" says Erna, then laughs.

"I was fifteen on the 22nd day of November and married on the 29th day," she says, recalling her brief courtship and long marriage with David Horton, a timberman from Jack's Creek.

Married in 1910, they had their first child in September of 1911. Together they raised nine of the ten children born to them. They lost one of a pair of twins born in 1923 but miraculously saved the other, a tiny girl who weighed a pound and a half at birth.

"My good Lord helped me raise her. She looked like a poor little bird. You could fold up a handkerchief, and it would make a good diaper for her. We didn't have no blankets, so I wrapped her up in a big old skirt.

"At night I'd take her to bed and lay her tiny head next to my cheek, so I could feel if she moved. When she was just three months old, I stayed up twenty-one nights, never laid down when she was sick. We laid her out once, thought she was dead," says Erna, then smiles across the room where the pound-and-a-half baby is now a seventy-three-year-old woman, Emmie Tapp.

"The Lord saved her to help take care of me later," says Erna, while her daughter ducks her head and blushes.

Raising children went right along with working for Erna and her husband. When they went to cut timber on Unaka Mountain, the young couple took their children into the woods with them, cleared a spot under a tree, chased away the copperheads and rattlesnakes, and told the little boys and girls to sit there while they worked.

"What we told them to do, they listened. Most times you could just look at them, they'd know what to do. Nowadays, the parents are obeying the children," says Erna.

She and David cut timber together. Each took an end of the long crosscut saw and went to work.

"I cut timber just like a man, cut great big, old, high chestnut trees. If they were twenty-five-thirty foot, we sawed them out for telephone poles, then we'd saw the rest up into five foot blocks and bust them.

"Then David would take it to Poplar with the horses to sell," she says, adding, "I was big and stout back then. I loved to work."

Gardening, raising stock and children, cooking, and cleaning left few hours for rest, but Erna and her family thrived in the frame house in Bailey Settlement. Today her daughter Emmie stays with her to help her, and another daughter Frankie Barnett lives just above the house and spends time caring for her, too.

Erna's blindness prevents her from walking through the gardens and tending the flowers, but she is still a vigorous presence in the house. Her daughters help her out onto the porch where she sits on a gliding sofa and slowly rocks, enjoying the warm summer afternoon.

She has learned much in her 101 years of life.

"You know, if you trust the Lord and depend on Him, He'll help us. I never could have gone through everything without Him. The Lord has been good to me," she says.

The original brick school building was torn down in 1960.

TIPTON HILL HIGH SCHOOL

From the 1920s to the 1960s in Tipton Hill, an isolated mountain community in Mitchell County, education flourished at a small local high school.

Separating fact from fiction and truth from stereotype has always been a problem in assessing life in the Southern Appalachians. A close look at the education provided at Tipton Hill High School for many years reveals that these Appalachian students, while they may have been money-poor, were by no means ignorant and uneducated.

From the beginning the community provided the drive to educate their children. With help from the Methodist Church, residents raised the funds to construct the first building, a two-story brick structure begun in 1921.

The school year 1923-24 saw the first classes held in the

school, which ran from first grade to high school. Previously classes had been held in a local church. In August 1924, the Mitchell County School Board purchased the school and began to maintain it.

By 1930 the school offered a variety of courses and a quantity of equipment that astonishes anyone who has been exposed to the stories of the squalor and ignorance prevalent in the isolated mountains. The *Tipton Hill-Billy*, a student newspaper published on March 28, 1930, presents a picture of involved, enthusiastic students and teachers in up-to-date interaction.

One article states, "There has been a moving picture show at the school building every two weeks since Christmas. The films have been furnished by the State Department of Education at Raleigh and we have enjoyed some splendid programs."

The senior class was busy rehearsing the play *A Noble Outcast* by John A. Frazer, Jr. The newspaper applauds the production for "its intense dramatic interest, a powerful sympathetic appeal, and the refined comedy which runs

Stone building built by WPA is today a sewing factory.

throughout the play."

In academics, three Tipton Hill students, Etta Frances, Carrie Canipe, and Abbie Canipe had submitted papers to the State French Contest at the University of North Carolina in Chapel Hill. Also Grace Tilley had won "honorable mention" for an article submitted to *Current Science* magazine.

"This means that her answer to the question, 'Why are bubbles always round?' was one of the twelve best in the whole United States and Canada," the article proudly states.

The newspaper also mentions the installation of the General Science, Biology, and Physics laboratory equipment that gave the school "the best equipped and most up-to-date science laboratory in the county."

In a short piece on "Styles" the paper reveals that "Most of them are not of the Parisian styles. . . . Most all the girls wear black or woolen sweaters with their print dresses. The boys wear overalls or dark trousers and sweaters with the large T's to represent the school."

In 1938 the WPA (Work Projects Administration) constructed a rock building to serve the high school students, leaving the elementary grades to occupy the old brick structure.

"The men got $19 for two weeks work, and they had to furnish their own wheelbarrows. We were so overcrowded in 1939. It was fortunate that they were able to bring us over to the new building," says Frank Griffith, who graduated from Tipton Hill High School in 1941.

From his store across the street, Griffith can see the rock building through which his class became the first to progress to graduation. Today it is a factory used by Taylor Togs.

The course of instruction during Griffith's time was impressive. He remembers Biology, Physics, Algebra 1 and 2, Literature, French, English, Home Economics ("for the girls"), Agriculture and Shop ("for the boys"), Typing, History, and General Science.

"When I look back at it now, I realize that the teachers had to do a tremendous amount of work," says Griffith, when he mentions that there were only four teachers at the time.

Freshman class 1937-38

During his student days, the school first began to serve lunch, a hot bowl of soup for ten cents.

"If you didn't have the money, you could trade produce for your lunch. A lot of the children brought in potatoes or canned vegetables to trade," says Griffith, who fondly remembers his days in the rock building.

He recalls that there was no such thing as snow days back then.

"One time we stayed in school until it was twenty-three inches deep. A bus driver tried to get the principal to turn out school when it had reached seventeen inches, but he wouldn't do it," says Griffith, putting his hand above his knee to show the depth of the snow.

With war coming on, the school year 1941-42 saw the addition of a teacher to bring the number of instructors to five. Culver Dale taught the boys aeronautics to prepare them for service to their country.

"Times was hard back then. A lot of boys left. Some went to CCC camps; some went to the service," says Griffith.

After the war Tipton Hill High School continued to educate the area youth. Marshall Street, a Buladean, North Carolina, sawmill operator, attended the school from 1948 to 1952. Although he had never played basketball before, he became a star on the school's team—because of his jumping ability.

"I had never seen the game till I played it. We played in a wood-frame gym sat out by the school. It was small, but it weren't too small," says Street, recalling the years of play on the hardcourt under coach A. D. Harrell, who had graduated from the school.

Street also drove the school bus from Buladean to Tipton Hill during his junior year. He carried about twenty students to the school on a bus that was not climate controlled.

"There wasn't no heater on it, and I froze to death. In the summer it would burn you up," he says, then laughs.

By the time he was in school, the lunchroom served full dinners. "They had different things. They had good food," he says.

While Marshall Street attended Buladean Elementary School for eight years before going over to Tipton Hill for the four years of high school, many students went through all twelve grades at Tipton Hill. Paul Bennett, who graduated in 1964 near the end of the high school's existence, began in 1952 in the elementary program.

Bennett, a well-known Mitchell County preacher and businessman, remains enthusiastic about his years at the small school. When the county consolidated high schools after 1967, he feels that a wonderful institution was lost.

"Even though it was out in a rural, isolated area, the quality of education at Tipton Hill surpassed the education of just about everywhere. People from the community came in and supported the school, had a lot of pride in it," says Bennett, who organized a reunion in November 1996 for all the school's graduates from 1929 to 1967.

He runs down a list of graduates who went on to become doctors, lawyers, evangelists, educators, and dentists, as well as well as citing numerous graduates who still live and work in the area. Their Tipton Hill education has carried them as far as they have wanted in life, providing a solid foundation that each has built upon according to his ambition.

Bertha Yelton, who taught at Tipton Hill High School for twenty-nine years, holds a carved horse.

BERTHA YELTON

Probably no on knows more about Tipton Hill High School than Bertha Yelton, who taught there for twenty-nine years. She arrived fresh from Berea College in 1937, increasing the staff from three to four teachers, and stayed throughout the rest of the school's existence.

A mountain girl herself, "a black diamond from West Virginia," she was at first surprised by the school's isolation. In fact, she found that Mitchell County was terra incognita to most people. When the county school superintendent told her to come to Toecane, she couldn't find anyone who knew where that was.

"I got as far as Johnson City. I couldn't find anybody there at night who knew where Toecane was. I had to spend the night in a hotel, and early next morning I got a taxi. He took me all the way around by Elk Park to Bakersville to the Superintendent's Office.

"It cost me $15, and I only made $90 a month," she says, looking back sixty years to when she was still Bertha Romansky.

Superintendent Bob Phillips found a young man to drive her to Tipton Hill from Bakersville.

"Bob Phillips was not only an educator; he was a matchmaker. That young man turned out to be my husband two years later," says Bertha Yelton, remembering the ride on curving mountain roads that left her physically ill and emotionally scared.

At the school she regularly taught Home Economics, General Science, and Biology each year. She also alternated Physics with Geometry every other year so the students could take both courses.

One year when a teacher left, she found herself teaching French, which she had studied at Berea College. She also taught English Literature and the History course when necessary and was put in charge of the Glee Club. Then there was Art.

"As a sideline, every teacher taught Art of some form. I had difficulty with a straight line, but I had had a course at Berea doing wood carving and folk dancing. I worked the carving in with my Biology class to get examples of each species of animal life," she says, taking down from her shelves a beautifully carved horse.

During the war she had to teach a compulsory course in Health to prepare the boys for war service. By the time the school closed for consolidation, there were six teachers.

"My husband was angry about consolidation. And one teacher left rather than consolidate. The main thing was that they'd have more equipment to work with. There was some truth in that.

"I had a much more beautiful room to work in and a nice Home Economics lab. But when you have students flowing through your hands so fast, you just don't get to know them. You get to know them much better when you have fewer of them," she says.

In the summer of 1996, students from the class of 1946 gathered in Johnson City, Tennessee, for their fiftieth reunion. They sent their former teacher a letter:

"At that time we had no paved roads, no telephones or televisions in that section of the country, school supplies were limited but immediately Miss Romansky went to work using what she had at hand and improving what she saw. . . .

"We know now what she guided us and taught us what was best; . . . Mrs. Yelton, you have done your job well; you helped to pour the foundation and lay the blocks, one by one, for many students. Now for many of us, the building is complete."

When she received and read the letter, Bertha Yelton got tears in her eyes. Such recognition rewarded her for the many years of dedicated teaching. It helps to explain how a small country high school turned out so many successful students.

Hannah Bennett's painting reveals the beauty of her mountain environment.

HANNAH BENNETT

Hannah Bennett has lived all of her eighty-plus years near the head of Brummett's Creek deep in the mountains of Mitchell County. While tramping through the forests along the steep slopes has always been her favorite occupation, painting vivid pictures and writing inspiring gospel songs have spread her vision of God's bounty throughout the country.

"I've always lived up here. I was born right over there in a two-room house. I've just stayed with it, because there is no place like home," she says, sitting at the old upright piano in her living room.

Warming herself by her woodstove after a cold morning at church, Hannah Bennett tells of her fifty years of married life with Edd Bennett, who passed on fourteen years ago.

"We got married in 1930 or '31. Edd and I had a jubilee for fifty years. We got along, and we enjoyed it. We'd go fishing to Lake James or Lake Watauga, or we'd walk through the mountains," she says, then smiles at the memories still fresh.

They never had a television or a radio. Perhaps that's why she had time to develop her talents.

"My husband would tell people I was a natural-born artist, and I guess I was," she says.

Hannah plays and sings one of her songs.

"I use oil all the time. I used to use watercolors, but somehow or other they just didn't please me. Most of the time I use canvas. That one there is canvas on plywood," she says, pointing to a painting of a house on a river.

Then she rises to get one of her oldest paintings. She returns with a picture of Jesus Christ that she painted over fifty years ago. The image came to her in a vision, and she painted it for herself.

"It was just for me," she says, holding up the vivid picture showing Christ with the crown of thorns piercing his high forehead over shining brown eyes. "For Me" is written across the bottom of the picture.

Hannah does not have many of her paintings. She sells

Hannah Bennett's visionary portrait of Jesus was painted fifty years ago.

most of them as soon as she paints them. People who have seen her work come to her with requests, which she fulfills, then they carry off the finished work of art.

She doesn't have a regular outlet for her paintings. People come by her house and see one, or they ask her to paint a special scene. She sets her paint board up on the piano, gets out her oils, and goes to work.

"Generally they pay me, but sometimes I give them away. I don't get no fortune out of it. I don't charge much, since it was a gift from God," she says, modestly bowing her head.

The grown children of one large family each wanted a picture of their homeplace on Pigeon Roost. Some wanted it showing the way the house was when they were children; others wanted it to appear as it was in the present. She painted two of one kind and four of the other.

"I have pictures pretty near all over the United States. I've been painting ever since I can remember. I painted one when I was about four or five years old. I painted a girl, and she had a rose. I tried to make a rose border," she says, then points out a picture hanging facing her front door.

The picture is of a Biblical scene—a river near Jerusalem. It glows with an other-worldly light that seems to shine from the scene itself.

"It came to me one day that I wanted to paint. I sat down and went to painting. I never did see that country, so I don't know if it's right or not. I just paint what I see in my mind," she says.

Music comes to her in the same way. Hannah has published several gospel songs, music that comes to her from God.

"I don't fool with any other kind, because I'm trying my best to get to a better world. All my loved ones are there, and I don't care at all to go there myself," says Hannah, as she turns around on her piano bench and starts to play and sing one of her compositions:

"When I am sad and feeling low,
And I find naught but grief and woe,
When I'm alone, no friend can see,
Then I hear Christ speaking to me.
God's holy word is in my heart,
And whenever the teardrops start,
Although his form I cannot see,
I can hear Him speaking to me."

Her voice rings strong and true above the tinkling piano, as she bobs her gray hair with the tune. Her brown eyes sparkle behind her thick glasses as she finishes her song:

"Come unto me and I'll give you rest,
Then I am so supremely blessed.
Although his form I cannot see,
I can hear Him speaking to me."

Her publisher is pleased with Hannah's work, but Hannah is not so pleased with her publisher. He took the liberty of changing the ending on one of her songs, so Hannah got all the copies she could and changed it to her original in pen and ink.

"They ended it on a high 'do,' and there isn't anybody who can sing that, so I just changed it back," she says, showing a copy of the sheet music.

With her two Samoyed dogs, Hannah is content to live her life on Brummett's Creek. Although she can't tramp for miles as she once could, she can still travel far enough into the forest to feel at home.

When she is tired or the weather too inclement, she sits at her piano and communes with God. Then she passes on her vision in music or paint.

Ron Townsend with Tobe, sorrel jack.

MULES

Mules—they are a much maligned species. Such cliches as "stubborn as a mule" paint them with a black brush. And even the donkey half of their parentage is used as a term of scorn, "asinine." There is much more to the mule than such disdain.

Mules—they are an enduring piece of our mountain heritage. From small, sure-footed hunting mules to the large draft animals, these sturdy beasts have served in a variety of roles ever since the white man entered the Southern Appalachians. While they are still the favorite of some mountain farmers, knowledge of mules is no longer common among most folks.

"A lot of people are unknowing about mules. Even some older people don't know a mule can't breed," says Ron

Townsend, a mule fancier and breeder who lives in a cove between Roan Mountain and Hampton.

Mules are hybrids, crosses between donkeys and horses, the asinine and the equine species. As hybrids, mules are sterile, both male and female, although there are stories of mare mules' having foals. Townsend claims that perhaps one mare in a thousand is fertile, while Cleo Edwards, who lives near Carver's Gap in Mitchell County and is a longtime horse and mule master, thinks the odds are even greater.

"I'd say it's closer to one in 2,000. It's a real rare thing for a mare mule to have a foal," says Edwards, hitching up his overall galluses.

Mules are the product of the mating of a donkey jack and a horse mare. The offspring of a horse stallion and a donkey jennet or jenny is a hinny.

"The most popular is the mule. Hardly ever see anyone go for a hinny," says Townsend, as he leads the way to his barn to show his jacks.

Townsend has three jacks, two black ones and a sorrel. You know that there is something different in that barn when

Lightning, mule filly eats beside her mother, a Clydesdale.

you hear the raucous blasts of the jacks. "Hee-haw! Hee-haw!" gives a poor idea of the actual sounds that emerge from the jackass. The series of squeeking honks proves that God has a sense of humor.

As Townsend leads Black Jack past the sorrel jack, Tobe, the latter frantically bites the top board of the gate to his stall, his eyes rolled back in his head. He's mad.

"Talk about fighting, they'll get into it, try to kill each other. I've heard of jacks killing a stallion — grab the horse on the throat and suffocate him," says Townsend as he rushes Black Jack out the barn door.

Black Jack, Tobe, and Bart, their stablemate, are jacks that Townsend uses for breeding. Folks come from miles around to have their mares bred by one of his jacks. Townsend is the local expert on mules, having bred, raised, and worked them most of his life.

He is even something of a scholar about mules.

"Did you know that in Biblical times royalty rode mules? Soldiers road horses, and the poor rode donkeys. But royalty rode mules. Mules are more sure-footed. They ride good.

"George Washington was one of the first mule breeders in this country. The Marquis de Lafayette gave him a large jack and some jennies. Other kings gave him jacks, too. He crossed them. He upgraded the mule quality and breed here in the United States," says Townsend as he shows his jack, pointing out the outstanding traits.

The first thing you notice is the ears. To say they are long is to be gentle. It is no wonder hunters have mistaken donkeys for giant jack rabbits at times. The ears are also extremely mobile, moving independently like those of indoor TV antennae.

Their tails are not bushy like a horse's, and their hooves are narrow and small. In temperament the ass is less flighty, more patient and sure-footed, and has more endurance than a horse. These traits are passed on to the mules.

One of Tobe's offspring is just across the state line in Avery County. Jack Jones bred his Clydesdale mare to the sorrel jack to get a sorrel filly, Lightning. The young mule is

Ron Townsend holds Black Bart.

closely watched by her mother and grandmother, both large mares descended from a brood mare Townsend had several years ago.

Already some of the characteristics of the mule are clearly developed. The thin legs and small hooves give her a dainty appearance, while the face and ears complete the donkey inheritance. The body shape, neck, and size come from the Clydesdale mother.

"Mules are a lot more sturdy than horses, a lot less prone to disease. They are less apt to founder (eat too much grain) — they won't eat enough to hurt theirselves. They are more sure-footed and don't get frustrated like a horse will.

"They have better endurance, and you can get over steeper ground with them than you can with horses. I kept teams until just a few years ago, did all my plowing and mowing. I mowed that steep side over there," says Townsend, pointing to a radically tilted pasture across the cove.

While Townsend plans to breed another mule team, across the Roan in Mitchell County, Cleo Edwards recently bought himself a young team of sorrel mare mules to work his land near the crest of the balds.

"They're the awfullest pets—right in your pockets all the time. Can't get them out of your pockets. I'm going to work them if my hands will let me loose, got the arthritis in them," he says, holding up his hands as the young pair nose around him.

"They're the finest little fellers ever was. So far they've done just exactly what I've asked them to. I've had the saddles on them and harnessed them," says Edwards as he places their bridles on the mules to get them used to them.

Maud and Molly make a pretty, matched team. Their sorrel coats gleam in the sun, and they have intelligent faces. They are lively and inquisitive, yet well-behaved.

"One is two this month, and the other will be two next month. Did he tell you he can take a pair of dog-clippers and shear the inside of their ears and they're just as calm?" says Edna Edwards, Cleo's wife who has ridden and worked alongside him under Grassy Ridge Bald for many years.

"He's got a whistle. All he has to do is blow a whistle and they'll come a-flying," she says.

When Cleo removes the bridles, the mules nuzzle at his pockets to see if he has any treats for them. As he leaves the pasture, they paw at the gate to have some more fun.

"You come back in a month or two, and I'll show you how they work," says Cleo, as he looks over them one more time and gives them each an affectionate rub before going to the house.

Don't even think "stubborn" or "asinine" around here.

Cleo and Edna Edwards begin harnessing Molly and Maude.

CLEO EDWARDS

Cleo Edwards lives in the same house where he was born on January 7, 1930, in Mitchell County, North Carolina. The beautiful balds of the Roan Highlands on the Tennessee-North Carolina border have formed his horizon and have been his playground his entire life. While the ancient mountains have a solid permanence that defies time, Cleo and his wife, Edna, have seen many changes come to their homeland.

A simple way of life has passed, although they keep much of it alive in practice, and all in memory. They are some of the last of those who find contentment in a life that assumes a comforting pattern dictated by the seasons. Constant growth is not their goal, but a reassuring repetition of a sustaining cycle that brings steady, known rewards.

"I was born in this old bunk, right where I am right now,"

says Cleo, gesturing around the snug kitchen of his frame house. His conversation is punctuated by the family dogs scratching to be let in or out of the screen door.

Edna was born nearby on Laurel Ridge, a spur of Roan Mountain, famous for its natural Catawba rhododendron gardens.

"I was born there, but that fall they moved to the top of Roan Mountain, right up on top in the gardens. My dad was working in the balsams. The first winter of my life was spent right on top of the mountain. You must have been four years old," she says, looking over to Cleo, who was old enough to remember what was happening on the Roan then.

"They had camps up there, real good camp buildings. They were timbering the balsam, hauled it off the mountain to where Herbert Gouge is. They had a tool—drawing knives—to shave the bark off it, then they'd haul it to Canton to the paper mill," says Cleo, as he pours hot water on the instant coffee in his cup.

In those days, people had come in from outside to help in the work. A good many found their way to the Roan balds

Cleo Edwards walks alongside Molly as she pulls the sled to the barn.

from the Great Smokies, where they had been bought out by the government.

"A lot of people came in here to work. Mark Jenkins, he was run out of the Smokies when they took the land there. His family had a camp off Carver's Gap. Most of them that left the Smokies came up here—something just about what they had before.

"They're all dead and gone, now," says Cleo, pausing to sip his coffee and remember the rugged mountain folks that formed his childhood.

Cleo and Edna attended local schools, Cleo finishing through eighth grade at nearby Glen Ayre at the foot of the mountain and Edna going on through high school at Bowman in Bakersville. Sturdy busses hauled them up and down the rough road that ran from the top of the Roan, through Glen Ayre, then on down to the county seat at Bakersville.

"The first school was down here at Glen Ayre, right across from where Thomas's building is. I went there the first year. The second it burnt down. I went on to Fork Mountain," says Cleo.

"There's always been a gravel road to the top of the mountain," says Edna, who bends to watch a ruby-throated hummingbird sip from the feeder hanging outside the kitchen window.

"A dad-burned old gravel road you could hardly get over, but the bus would run," says Cleo, reaching to open the door for a portly beagle.

The road evokes more than memories of going to school. Road work by the Depression-created WPA to keep the road in shape caused some problems for the Edwards family.

"We had the prettiest bed of corn, down there where the lily place is. They came off the bank and started pulling it off and chopping it. My daddy was pretty dad-gummed upset. We needed that corn.

"I was maybe six-year-old. I remember them digging our corn up because I was picking beans in it. After my daddy talked with them, they skipped that place and waited till the fall to work on the bank," says Cleo.

The Depression years, which brought misery to most of the country, didn't greatly affect the isolated community on the Roan. They never had much cash, before or during the thirties, but they always had plenty of food.

"I never in my life ever remember going hungry. We'd raise us sheep and raise us a couple of hogs. We had a cow for milk and butter. We growed all our feed. We had corn for meal. The only thing we'd buy was coffee, a little bit of sugar. . . ," says Cleo.

"And flour," adds Edna.

"And flour. The rest of it we raised ourselves," says Cleo.

Along with the abundant food went hard work—but work that Cleo enjoyed.

"From the time I was about eight year old I started driving a team. I had to have me a box to stand on to put the harness on. From the time I was big enough to reach the plow handles, I'd plow," he says, looking at his hands, hardened by years of gripping driving lines or smooth-worn plow handles.

Working horses was Cleo's first real job. It began by chance.

"Lee Gouge had a big pair of black horses. One would kick your head off if you weren't careful. One Monday morning I was over where he was cutting timber, and one of his drivers didn't come in. I was about twelve year old. I said I could do it.

"I started pulling those logs at a dollar a day. I pulled two days at the sawmill, then I went to the woods with them. I could work just as well as anyone else," says Cleo, looking out the window over the ridge where the logging occurred.

"They sawed it straight across the hill from me. There was as good a cherry timber as you ever saw. There was a lot of oak, water oak, sugar trees, ash, and some big old beech timber. They worked there a couple of years," he says.

One of the changes he has seen is the disappearance of the valuable timber which was cut from that forest.

"None of the real pretty sugar trees and ash and cherry ever came back. It all grew up in beech, and that beech, it

Cleo Edwards

just ain't no good for much," he says.

Cleo remembers the large engine that they used to saw the timber once it had been pulled from the woods by the horse teams, and how they got it to the site.

"They had to build a bridge over the creek. At first they couldn't pull it, so they put six head to it. That's the first six-horse hitch I've ever seen," he says.

Cleo has remained a horsemaster throughout his life, raising, training, and working horses and mules to work his twenty-nine-acre farm and to work throughout the mountains logging.

Another way he earned money was collecting bark, herbs, and roots to sell. He roamed the mountains with his friend Herbert Gouge collecting angelica, may apple, blood root, and cherry bark.

"We pulled may apple, easiest stuff you've ever dug. You'd have a main big bushel of it. By the time it dries, you won't have a pound. Then I've skinned cherry bark, me and Herbert Gouge.

"There was a guy lived on Red Hill or Tipton Hill—Charlie Whitson—he'd come about every Wednesday in a pickup. He'd buy old chickens, ginseng, anything you'd have for sale. I've spent hours waiting for him," says Cleo.

For recreation Cleo and his younger brother had the whole Roan massif. Hunting, running coons, and riding the livestock left to summer on the balds filled the little leisure time he had. The beasts would be brought up in the middle of April and left until the middle of September by farmers for miles around. The abundant grasses would fatten even the leanest horse.

"Our Sunday hobby for me and my brother was to go up and catch horses and ride 'em. We'd ride anything we could catch, the wildest and hardest. Mules, oxen and horses we'd ride.

"There was a little blue, mouse-colored mule—now, you didn't ride him. He put us off every time we'd get on," says Cleo, a smile crossing his face as he remembers the excitement of the impromptu rodeos.

Today there is no horse-riding on the balds. The only livestock pastured there are grass-cutting goats inside electric fences. The herds are herds of tourists puffing up from Carver's Gap. Farms have gone to tourist houses, and pastures have grown up.

But Cleo and Edna have a new team of mules they are training. Blackberries are ripening, the garden's producing, and the dogs are going in and out the screen door. At the Edwards, things haven't changed so much.

Grave site of C. Rex Peake lies under Grassy Ridge Bald.

C. REX PEAKE

He took his last trip
Up the mountain today.
Friends and neighbors
walked softly the way—
I cannot think that he is there.
My eyes will lift to find him where
The wind blows free
In grass and tree.
"Bury me on top of the Roan," he said,
And though they tell me he is dead,
There's doubt in every tone.
We laid him halfway to the top,
But somehow I think he didn't stop.
He's still on his own adventurous way—
Unafraid, confident, searching, and gay.

Sarah Cannon Spell

On the crest of Grassy Ridge Bald in the Roan massif several large granite boulders lie. For hundreds—perhaps thousands—of years, men who have reached the top of that beautiful bald have stood on the topmost boulder to see the highlands and the valleys below stretching to the horizon.

Today on that boulder is fixed a large bronze plaque. It says:

To honor the memory of
Cornelious Rex Peake

A special man who loved God, his country, his fellow men and this land: a legacy from his forefathers.

Born in the valley below, April 3, 1887, buried near his birthplace, March 23, 1964. Because of his love of nature, his long and close association with this mountain, no one was better versed on the Roan and it's [sic] people."

On the plaque are also included the above verses from a memorial poem by Sarah Cannon Spell and a rhododendron blossom and some Fraser fir trees, symbols of the mountain's natural beauty.

C. Rex Peake wanted to be buried on the top of Grassy Ridge Bald. The mountain was both his home and his living from his birth.

"It was just his life. That's all," says Cleo Edwards, who knew C. Rex Peake for fifty years, working and playing with him on the slopes of the mountain they both loved.

"I helped him up there one day. We set four pieces of bridging steel. Drove that steel down there where he wanted to be buried. It's right there where his plaque's at," he says, leaning back in his chair and thinking back to that day.

When the time came for Peake's burial, the weather forbade his body's being taken to the top of the mountain, so he was buried below the peak on a small knoll in a pasture. The grave is not far from his birthplace.

"He was born about twenty yard out from the grave, in an old log house. He showed me where it was at," says Cleo.

Grassy Ridge Bald looms over the pasture where Peake's grave lies next to that of his wife, enclosed in a graying, split-locust fence. The ever changing vista of mist and clouds and mountain moving through the four seasons surrounds the enclosure.

Grassy Ridge Bald stands in its natural beauty of waving grass, dark green rhododendron bushes and fir trees, and permanent gray granite. In season there are the purple-red blossoms of the Catawba rhododendron, the glowing orange blossoms of the Gray's lily, the small blue blossoms of the bluets, and the yellow-to-orange flames of the azalea.

"He wanted it left just like it was. He kept his cattle up there. And Lord, I've went up there with him—we'd go up there, just walk straight up the pasture.

"We'd bring his cattle off and vaccinate them for black leg and take them back. I've went with him many a day," says Cleo, looking out his kitchen window up to Grassy Ridge Bald that closes his horizon.

C. Rex Peake wrote a book on the Roan. It was simply entitled *Roan Mt.* On the cover is a rough line drawing of the

Grassy Ridge Bald was Peake's livelihood and playground.

road to Carver's Gap, and the humps of the balds stretching on either side.

In it he writes: "This is one of the oldest and most beautiful mountains in the world."

Peake describes the topography of the massif and briefly covers the mountain's history from its being the site of a battle between the Cherokee and Catawba Indian tribes, to its development as a resort with the Cloudland Hotel.

He writes of the various kinds of rhododendron, and "some rare flowers and plants, such as Gray's lily, which was found by Asa Gray in 1841, and is not found elsewhere.

"Also there is Scotch heather, (found only in Scotland and the Appalachian Mountains), wild geranium, Greenland chickweed, bluets (forget-me-nots) and purple fringed orchids. Other flowering plants make this mountain a botanist's paradise."

Peake also describes some unique local mountain folks, such as Uncle Starling. The six-foot-four-inch Starling with a number twelve size boot lived a perfectly normal life for fifty-five years. Then for four years he lost his mind trying to figure out where God was and what he was doing before he created the universe.

Then he returned to normal. He described his release to Peake:

"'One day, I was up thar at the Elk Holler looking up wer sheep and wer cattle, and it came the awfulest storm I ever seed. I run under them thar shelving rocks, thar where you turn down to Heaton Creek, and the thunder and the lightning was a cracking and popping all around.

"'And thar I was a-wondering whar God come from. All of a sudden thunder struck a big sugar tree in about ten feet of me, throwed bark splinters all over me and I decided it was just none of my business where God come from. That he was right thar, and could have killed me, and I just snapped out of her and was well again.'

"He lived a normal life for the rest of his days, age 89," concludes Peake.

His pamphlet was sold at the Roan View Gift Shop located

Memorial plaque is fixed to boulder near wher Peake wanted to be buried.

just down from Carver's Gap on the North Carolina side. His wife, Winnie, and her friend Grace Pack Durham ran the small souvenir shop, that stands in ruins today.

"Grace and Winnie set it up and worked it," says Cleo, then breaks into a chuckle.

"One year Rex and I made maple sugar. Up above the barn there was a spot that I said it'd be a good spot for a furnace, a good place to boil it off. We made about eighty-five gallons.

"He had to hide his. He said that if he took it to the house, Winnie would put it in pint bottles and sell it at that gift shop," says Cleo, demonstrating how Winnie Peake would pour syrup into the small jars.

Cleo has lots of stories about C. Rex Peake. Some can be told and some can't. There was the time his hay rake tongue broke, and Rex fell under the rake and was rolled over and over down the mountain. What he said to the horse remains Cleo's secret.

And the time he found a vein of quartz in Cleo's pasture and returned with a rock hammer and pick to strike it rich, until Cleo had to stop him because he was putting big holes in the pasture.

"There wasn't nothing you could ask Rex to do but he wouldn't come help," says Cleo, remembering the man who spent his life on the mountain he loved.

When the government went to court to get Grassy Ridge Bald from the Peake heirs, part of the purchase agreement was that a permanent memorial to Rex Peake would be placed on the mountain.

The granite rocks on Grassy Ridge Bald are no more permanent than C. Rex Peake's love for his mountain. When you see the plaque, pause to remember the man who preserved the mountain he loved.

max hopson
frank whitson
stanleys
campbell
genual wilder
frank mosley
milan street